Swift Essentials: A Comprehensive Guide to iOS App Development

Kameron Hussain and Frahaan Hussain

Published by Sonar Publishing, 2023.

SWIFT ESSENTIALS: A COMPREHENSIVE GUIDE TO IOS APP DEVELOPMENT

First edition. October 28, 2023.

ISBN: 979-8223120520

Written by Kameron Hussain and Frahaan Hussain.

Table of Contents

Core Data provides a robust and efficient way to manage and persist data in your iOS app. It's particularly useful when dealing with complex data structures, relationships, and querying requirements. By using Core Data, you can create scalable and maintainable data-driven apps with ease.

1. Unit Testing and Test Coverage
2. Integration Testing
3. Continuous Integration (CI)
4. Performance Testing
5. Crash Reporting
6. Beta Testing
7. User Acceptance Testing (UAT)
8. Automated UI Testing
9. Code Reviews
10. Security Auditing
11. Documentation
12. Version Control
13. Error Monitoring
14. Performance Monitoring
15. User Feedback
16. Regression Testing

Chapter 16: App Distribution and Deployment

Section 16.1: Preparing Your App for Submission

1. Code Review and Cleanup
2. Testing and Debugging

8. App Store Review Submission

9. App Review Status

10. App Release and Distribution

11. Monitoring App Performance

12. App Updates

13. App Store Optimization (ASO)

14. App Store Resources

Section 16.3: Managing App Versions and Updates

1. Versioning Your App

2. Updating App Information

3. Release Notes

4. Testing Updates

5. Version Compatibility

6. App Store Review Process

7. Updating Rejected Apps

8. Timely Updates

9. App Promotion

10. User Feedback

11. App Store Optimization (ASO)

12. Measuring Update Impact

7. Donations

8. Affiliate Marketing

9. Data Monetization

10. E-commerce Integration

Section 17.2: Implementing In-App Purchases

1. Set Up Your App in App Store Connect

2. Create IAP Products

3. Integrate StoreKit Framework

4. Handle IAP Transactions

5. Unlock Purchased Content

6. Restore Purchases

7. Test IAPs

8. Handle Receipt Validation

9. Comply with Apple's Guidelines

Section 17.3: Managing Subscriptions

1. Types of Subscriptions

2. Implementing Subscriptions

3. Subscription States

4. Receipt Validation

5. Subscription Management UI

Terms of Service and Privacy Policy

Security

Accessibility Compliance

Consult with Legal Experts

Section 18.5: Creating Inclusive iOS Apps

1. Understanding Accessibility Guidelines

2. Use Adaptive Layouts

3. VoiceOver Support

4. Dynamic Text and Font Adjustment

5. High Contrast and Dark Mode

6. Alternative Text for Images

7. Keyboard Navigation

8. Testing with Assistive Technologies

9. Accessible Multimedia

10. Avoid Exclusive Gestures

11. Support for Switch Control

12. Inclusive Design Thinking

13. Accessibility Labeling for Custom UI Elements

14. Accessibility Audits

15. User Education

1. Swift 1.0 (2014)
2. Swift 2.0 (2015)
3. Swift 3.0 (2016)
4. Swift 4.0 (2017)
5. Swift 4.2 (2018)
6. Swift 5.0 (2019)
7. Swift 5.1 (2019)
8. Swift 5.5 (2021)

Section 20.3: Trends in User Experience Design

1. Minimalism and Clean Interfaces
2. Dark Mode and Light Mode
3. Microinteractions
4. Gesture-Based Navigation
5. Personalization and AI
6. Accessibility and Inclusivity
7. Augmented Reality (AR) Integration
8. Sustainability and Ethical Design

Section 20.4: App Security and Privacy

1. Data Encryption
2. Secure Authentication

3. User Data Permissions

4. Secure Backend

5. Data Minimization

6. Privacy Policy

7. Regular Security Audits

8. User Consent

9. Legal Compliance

10. Data Breach Response Plan

Section 20.5: Building for the Future of iOS

1. Swift Evolution

2. Cross-Platform Development

3. Machine Learning and AI

4. Augmented Reality (AR)

5. IoT Integration

6. Privacy-Focused Design

7. App Clips

8. Accessibility and Inclusivity

9. Security

10. 5G Connectivity

11. Sustainability

12. User-Centric Design

Chapter 1: Getting Started with Swift and iOS Development

Section 1.1: Introduction to Swift

Swift is a powerful and versatile programming language developed by Apple for building applications on iOS, macOS, watchOS, and tvOS platforms. It was introduced in 2014 as a replacement for Objective-C, offering modern syntax, improved performance, and a more developer-friendly experience.

Key Features of Swift

Swift has gained popularity among developers for several reasons:

1. **Readability**: Swift's syntax is concise and easy to read, making code more understandable and maintainable.
2. **Safety**: Swift incorporates safety features like type inference, optionals, and memory management, reducing the risk of common programming errors.
3. **Performance**: Swift is designed for high performance, and its compiled code often runs faster than equivalent Objective-C code.
4. **Interoperability**: Swift can work seamlessly with Objective-C, allowing developers to use both languages within the same project.
5. **Open Source**: Swift is open-source, which means that developers can contribute to its improvement and port it to other platforms.

Getting Started with Swift

To start using Swift for iOS development, you'll need the following:

- **Xcode**: Xcode is Apple's integrated development environment (IDE) for macOS. It includes a code editor, debugger, and Interface Builder for designing user interfaces.

- **macOS**: You need a Mac running macOS to develop iOS apps because Xcode is only available on macOS.

- **Swift Language**: Swift comes bundled with Xcode, so you don't need to separately install it.

Your First Swift Program

Let's begin with a simple "Hello, World!" program in Swift:

```
import UIKit

func sayHello() {

print("Hello, World!")

}

sayHello()
```

In this code:

- We import the UIKit framework, which is essential for iOS development.

- We define a function sayHello() that prints "Hello, World!" to the console.

- Finally, we call the sayHello() function to execute it.

When you run this program in Xcode, you should see "Hello, World!" printed in the Xcode console.

Swift Playground

Xcode also provides a feature called "Playgrounds" where you can experiment with Swift code in an interactive environment. Playgrounds are excellent for learning Swift concepts, testing code snippets, and visualizing results.

In a playground, you can write Swift code and see the output immediately, making it a valuable tool for learning Swift and exploring its capabilities.

Conclusion

This brief introduction provides an overview of Swift and how to get started with your first Swift program. In the upcoming sections of this book, we will delve deeper into Swift programming and iOS development, building on these foundational concepts. So, let's continue our journey to become proficient iOS developers.

Section 1.2: Setting Up Xcode

Xcode is the primary integrated development environment (IDE) for iOS app development, and setting it up correctly is crucial to start building iOS applications. In this section, we will walk through the steps to set up Xcode on your macOS system.

Download and Install Xcode

1. **Apple ID**: Ensure that you have an Apple ID. If you don't have one, you can create it on the Apple ID website[1].

---

1. https://appleid.apple.com/

2. **App Store**: Open the App Store on your Mac and search for "Xcode." It's available for free. Click the "Get" button and follow the installation instructions.
3. **Updates**: Xcode and its components receive regular updates. After installation, periodically check for updates in the App Store to ensure you have the latest version.

Command Line Tools

Xcode includes command line tools that are essential for building and running iOS applications from the terminal. To install these tools, follow these steps:

1. **Open Terminal**: Launch the Terminal app on your Mac.
2. **Run the Command**: Enter the following command and press Enter:

```
xcode-select—install
```

1. **Installation Prompt**: A dialog box will appear, asking if you want to install the command line developer tools. Click "Install" and follow the on-screen instructions.

Launching Xcode

Once Xcode is installed, you can find it in your Applications folder or by searching for "Xcode" using Spotlight. Launch Xcode, and you'll be greeted with a welcome screen.

Xcode Preferences

Before you start developing, it's a good idea to configure some Xcode preferences to tailor the IDE to your needs. Here are a few settings to consider:

• **Themes**: Xcode offers both light and dark themes. You can choose your preferred theme in Xcode preferences under the "Themes" tab.

• **Key Bindings**: Customize keyboard shortcuts for various actions in the "Key Bindings" section of preferences.

• **Fonts and Colors**: Adjust the font size and colors in the "Fonts & Colors" section to make the code editor more comfortable for you.

• **Behaviors**: Customize how Xcode responds to specific events, such as build success or errors, in the "Behaviors" section.

Creating Your First Xcode Project

Now that Xcode is set up, you can create your first iOS project:

1. **Open Xcode**: Launch Xcode from your Applications folder.
2. **Create a New Project**: Click on "Create a new Xcode project" or use the "File" menu to start a new project.
3. **Choose a Template**: Xcode provides various project templates for different types of apps. Choose the one that best fits your project, and click "Next."
4. **Configure Your Project**: Give your project a name, specify where you want to save it, and configure other project settings.
5. **Create**: Click the "Create" button, and Xcode will generate the initial project files and open them for you to start coding.

With Xcode properly set up, you're ready to embark on your iOS development journey. In the subsequent sections of this book, we will explore the various aspects of iOS development, diving deeper into Swift, user interfaces, and app architecture.

Section 1.3: Creating Your First iOS Project

Now that you have Xcode installed and set up on your macOS system, it's time to create your first iOS project. In this section, we'll walk through the steps to create a simple "Hello, iOS" application to get you started with iOS app development.

Launching Xcode

1. **Open Xcode**: If you haven't already, open Xcode from your Applications folder or by using Spotlight search.
2. **Welcome Screen**: When Xcode opens, you'll see a welcome screen with options to create a new Xcode project or open an existing one. Click on "Create a new Xcode project."

Choosing a Template

1. **Select a Template**: Xcode provides various project templates for different types of iOS apps. For this example, we'll create a "Single View App," which is a simple iOS app with a single screen. Select the "iOS App" template and click "Next."
2. **Project Configuration**: You'll be prompted to configure your new project. Here's what each field means:

– **Product Name**: Enter a name for your app (e.g., "HelloiOS").

– **Organization Name**: Your organization's name or your own name.

– **Organization Identifier:** This is typically in reverse domain format (e.g., "com.example").

– **Bundle Identifier**: Xcode will automatically generate this based on your product name and organization identifier.

– **Language**: Choose "Swift" as the language for this project.

– **Use Core Data**: Leave this unchecked for now.

– **Include Unit Tests**: Make sure this option is selected.

– **Include UI Tests**: Also, ensure this option is selected.

1. **Save Location**: Choose where you want to save your project on your computer. You can leave it as the default location or specify a different one.
2. **Git**: If you use Git for version control, you can select "Create Git repository on my Mac" to initialize a Git repository for your project. This step is optional.

Creating Your Project

1. **Create:** After configuring your project, click the "Create" button. Xcode will generate the initial project files and open the project in the Xcode workspace.

Exploring the Project Structure

1. **Xcode Workspace**: In Xcode, you work within a workspace, which can contain multiple projects. The workspace allows you to manage dependencies between different parts of your app.
2. **Project Navigator**: On the left side of the Xcode window, you'll find the Project Navigator. It displays the structure of your project, including source code files, assets, and resources.
3. **Main.storyboard**: This is where you design the user interface of your app using Interface Builder. You can visually arrange UI elements and set their properties.
4. **ViewController.swift**: This is the Swift source code file for the initial view controller of your app. It controls the behavior and functionality of the app's user interface.

Running Your App

1. **Select a Simulator**: At the top left corner of the Xcode window, choose a device simulator to run your app on. You can select an iPhone or iPad simulator with different iOS versions.
2. **Run the App**: Click the "Run" button (a triangle icon) in the top-left corner of the Xcode window. Xcode will build your project and launch the app in the selected simulator.
3. **View Your App**: After a brief moment, the simulator will open, and you'll see your "Hello, iOS" app running. It's a simple blank screen for now, but it's your first iOS app!

Congratulations! You've successfully created and run your first iOS project in Xcode. In the upcoming sections, we'll dive deeper into iOS app development, including designing user interfaces, writing Swift code, and building more complex functionality.

Section 1.4: Exploring the Xcode Interface

As you embark on your iOS development journey, it's essential to become familiar with the Xcode Integrated Development Environment (IDE). Xcode provides a rich set of tools and features to streamline the development process. In this section, we'll explore the key elements of the Xcode interface to help you get comfortable with it.

Xcode Workspace

When you open Xcode, you work within a workspace. A workspace can contain one or more projects, making it easier to manage related code and assets. Workspaces are a fundamental part of organizing your development work.

Project Navigator

The Project Navigator is located on the left side of the Xcode window. It displays the structure of your project. Here are some essential elements within the Project Navigator:

- **Your Project**: At the top of the Project Navigator, you'll find the name of your project. This is the root of your project's file hierarchy.

- **Groups and Files**: Beneath your project name, you'll see folders and files. You can create groups to organize your files logically. Groups don't affect the actual file structure on disk; they are for organizational purposes.

- **Assets.xcassets**: This is where you manage your app's image assets, such as icons and launch screens.

- **Main.storyboard**: This is the visual interface builder for designing your app's user interface.

- **ViewController.swift**: The Swift source code file for the initial view controller of your app.

Editor Area

The Editor Area is the central part of the Xcode window where you write and edit code or work on Interface Builder files. It can display various editors, such as:

- **Code Editor**: This editor is used for writing Swift code. When you open a Swift file, it will appear in the code editor.

- **Interface Builder**: When you open a storyboard or XIB file, Xcode switches to Interface Builder mode, allowing you to design your app's user interface visually.

Toolbar

The Toolbar is located at the top of the Xcode window and provides quick access to commonly used actions and features. Some important toolbar elements include:

- **Run and Stop Buttons**: The "Run" button (a triangle) builds and runs your app in the simulator, while the "Stop" button (a square) terminates the app.

- **Scheme Selector**: The scheme defines how your app is built and run. You can choose different schemes for debugging, testing, or releasing your app.

- **Device Selector**: You can choose the target device (simulator or physical device) for running your app.

- **Editor Layout**: You can choose how the editors are arranged, including options for code and interface editors side by side.

Debug Area

The Debug Area appears at the bottom of the Xcode window when you run your app in debugging mode. It provides tools for inspecting variables, viewing console output, and analyzing the app's behavior while it's running.

Utilities and Inspectors

The Utilities area is on the right side of the Xcode window. It hosts various inspectors and utilities that allow you to modify properties of selected elements in Interface Builder, such as buttons or labels. You can also access file and project settings here.

Organizer

The Organizer is a separate window accessed from the Window menu or by pressing Shift+Cmd+2. It provides tools for managing your development assets, such as provisioning profiles, app archives, and devices.

Version Editor

The Version Editor is used for comparing different versions of your source code. It helps you track changes and manage code collaboration if you're using version control systems like Git.

Conclusion

Familiarizing yourself with the Xcode interface is the first step in becoming proficient in iOS development. As you work on your projects, you'll explore and use these different areas of Xcode extensively. In the upcoming chapters, we'll delve deeper into various aspects of iOS app development, including writing Swift code, designing user interfaces, and building functionality to create compelling iOS applications.

Section 1.5: Understanding the iOS Development Ecosystem

Before diving deeper into iOS development, it's essential to have a good understanding of the broader iOS development ecosystem. This section will provide an overview of the key components, technologies, and concepts that make up this ecosystem.

iOS Platform

iOS is the mobile operating system developed by Apple for its iPhones, iPads, and iPod Touch devices. It's known for its user-friendly interface, security features, and seamless integration with other Apple services and devices. iOS serves as the foundation for building and running iOS applications.

Xcode

As you've already learned, Xcode is the official Integrated Development Environment (IDE) for iOS app development. It provides tools for writing, testing, and debugging iOS applications. Xcode streamlines the development process by offering features like Interface Builder, a code editor, and debugging tools.

Swift Programming Language

Swift is the primary programming language used for iOS app development. It was introduced by Apple in 2014 to replace Objective-C. Swift is known for its modern syntax, safety features, and performance. It's an integral part of the iOS development ecosystem and is used to write the logic of iOS applications.

Interface Builder

Interface Builder is a graphical user interface design tool within Xcode. It allows you to visually design your app's user interface by dragging and dropping UI elements onto a canvas. You can set properties, define layout constraints, and connect UI elements to code using Interface Builder. This tool significantly simplifies the process of creating visually appealing and responsive user interfaces.

App Store

The Apple App Store is the official distribution platform for iOS applications. It provides a marketplace where users can discover, download, and install iOS apps on their devices. As an iOS developer, you'll need to understand the App Store submission process, including guidelines, app review, and distribution methods.

Developer Program

To publish your iOS apps on the App Store, you'll need to enroll in the Apple Developer Program. This program offers various membership levels, including the free Apple Developer account and the paid Apple Developer Program. Paid memberships provide additional benefits, such as app distribution, access to beta software, and more.

Testing and Debugging

Testing and debugging are critical aspects of iOS development. Xcode offers a suite of testing tools, including unit testing and UI testing frameworks, to ensure the quality and reliability of your apps. You'll also use debugging tools to identify and fix issues in your code.

Version Control

Version control is essential for managing and collaborating on iOS projects. Developers often use Git, a distributed version control system, to track changes in their code, collaborate with team members, and manage code repositories.

Libraries and Frameworks

The iOS development ecosystem includes a wide range of libraries and frameworks that simplify common tasks and provide pre-built functionality. For example, UIKit is a framework for building user interfaces, Core Data is used for data storage, and Core Location provides location services.

Community and Resources

The iOS developer community is vibrant and active. You can find numerous online resources, forums, blogs, and tutorials dedicated to iOS development. Platforms like Stack Overflow and GitHub are valuable for seeking help, sharing code, and collaborating with other developers.

Conclusion

Understanding the iOS development ecosystem is crucial for anyone looking to become an iOS developer. This ecosystem consists of the iOS platform itself, development tools like Xcode, the Swift programming language, and various resources and communities that support iOS developers. In the following chapters, we will dive deeper into these components, providing you with the knowledge and skills needed to create your own iOS applications.

Chapter 2: Swift Fundamentals

Section 2.1: Variables and Constants

In Swift, variables and constants are fundamental for storing and managing data. Understanding how to declare and use them is crucial as you start working with the Swift programming language. In this section, we'll explore variables, constants, and their usage in Swift.

Declaring Variables and Constants

You can declare a variable in Swift using the var keyword and a constant using the let keyword. Here's how you declare them:

```
var myVariable = 42 // This is a variable
```

```
let myConstant = "Hello, Swift!" // This is a constant
```

- Variables are mutable, meaning their values can change after initialization.

- Constants are immutable, and once assigned a value, they cannot be changed.

Type Annotations

Swift uses type inference to automatically determine the data type of a variable or constant based on the initial value. However, you can also specify the data type explicitly using a type annotation. Here's how:

```
var age: Int = 30 // Explicitly specifying Int
```

```
let pi: Double = 3.14159 // Explicitly specifying Double
```

Type Safety and Type Inference

Swift is a statically-typed language, which means that once you've declared a variable or constant with a particular type, you cannot assign values of different types to it. Type safety helps catch errors at compile-time rather than runtime.

var score: Int = 42

score = "Hello" *// Error: Cannot assign a value of type 'String' to a variable of type 'Int'*

Swift also uses type inference to deduce the data type of a variable or constant based on the assigned value. This makes the code cleaner and more concise:

var name = "John" *// Type inference: name is inferred to be of type String*

let temperature = 23.5 *// Type inference: temperature is inferred to be of type Double*

Naming Conventions

When naming variables and constants, adhere to Swift's naming conventions:

- Use descriptive names that reflect the purpose of the variable or constant.

- Start variable and constant names with a lowercase letter, and use camelCase (e.g., myVariable, studentName).

- Constants should be declared using all uppercase letters with underscores (e.g., MAX_VALUE, PI).

Printing Values

You can use the print() function to output the values of variables and constants to the console for debugging and testing purposes:

```
var age = 25

print(age) // Output: 25

let message = "Hello, Swift!"

print(message) // Output: Hello, Swift!
```

Conclusion

Variables and constants are the building blocks of Swift programming. They allow you to store and manage data in your applications. Understanding the differences between variables and constants, type annotations, type safety, and naming conventions is essential as you continue to learn Swift and develop iOS applications. In the upcoming sections, we'll explore data types, operators, control flow, and more Swift fundamentals.

Section 2.2: Data Types and Type Inference

Swift is a statically-typed language, which means that every variable and constant must have a specific data type. In this section, we'll explore Swift's built-in data types and how type inference simplifies variable declarations.

Basic Data Types

Swift provides a range of basic data types to work with different kinds of values:

• **Integers**: Used to represent whole numbers. Swift offers Int for signed integers and UInt for unsigned integers. Examples:

```
let age: Int = 30

let population: UInt = 8_000_000
```

• **Floating-Point Numbers**: Used to represent numbers with a fractional part. Swift offers Double for 64-bit floating-point numbers and Float for 32-bit floating-point numbers. Examples:

```
let pi: Double = 3.14159

let temperature: Float = 23.5
```

• **Booleans**: Used to represent true or false values. Swift has a Bool data type. Examples:

```
let isRaining: Bool = true

let isSunny: Bool = false
```

• **Strings**: Used to represent text. Swift's String type allows you to work with text and manipulate strings. Examples:

```
let greeting: String = "Hello, World!"

let name: String = "Alice"
```

Type Inference

Swift features type inference, which means you often don't need to explicitly specify a variable's data type. The compiler can automatically determine the type based on the initial value:

let age = 30 *// Compiler infers age as Int*

let pi = 3.14159 *// Compiler infers pi as Double*

let isRaining = **true** *// Compiler infers isRaining as Bool*

let greeting = "Hello, World!" *// Compiler infers greeting as String*

Type inference reduces redundancy in your code and makes it more concise. However, you can still specify data types explicitly when needed for clarity or when the compiler might not infer the correct type.

Type Aliases

Swift allows you to create custom type aliases using the typealias keyword. This can make your code more readable and maintainable:

typealias EmployeeID = Int

let employeeNumber: EmployeeID = 12345

In this example, we've defined an alias EmployeeID for the Int type, making it clear that employeeNumber represents an employee ID.

Type Safety

Swift's type safety ensures that you can't mix and match data types without explicit conversion. For example, you can't add an Int and a Double without converting one of them:

let intValue: Int = 5

let doubleValue: Double = 3.14

let sum = intValue + doubleValue *// Error: Cannot convert value of type 'Double' to expected argument type 'Int'*

You would need to convert one of the values to match the other's type explicitly.

Conclusion

Understanding Swift's data types and type inference is crucial for writing clean, reliable code. By leveraging type inference, you can make your code more concise while maintaining clarity. In the next sections, we'll explore operators and expressions, control flow, and more advanced Swift concepts to enhance your iOS development skills.

Section 2.3: Operators and Expressions

Operators are fundamental to performing operations on data in any programming language. Swift offers a wide range of operators for arithmetic, comparison, logical operations, and more. In this section, we'll explore Swift's operators and expressions.

Arithmetic Operators

Swift supports the standard arithmetic operators for performing mathematical operations on numeric values:

- **Addition** (+): Used to add two values together.
- **Subtraction** (-): Used to subtract the right operand from the left operand.

- **Multiplication (*)**: Used to multiply two values.

- **Division** (/): Used to divide the left operand by the right operand.

- **Remainder** (%): Used to calculate the remainder after division.

Here are some examples:

let x = 10

let y = 3

let sum = x + y *// 13*

let difference = x - y *// 7*

let product = x * y *// 30*

let quotient = x / y *// 3*

let remainder = x % y *// 1*

Compound Assignment Operators

Swift provides compound assignment operators that allow you to perform an operation and assign the result in a single step:

- +=: Adds the right operand to the left operand and assigns the result to the left operand.

- -=: Subtracts the right operand from the left operand and assigns the result to the left operand.

- *=: Multiplies the left operand by the right operand and assigns the result to the left operand.

• /=: Divides the left operand by the right operand and assigns the result to the left operand.

• %=: Calculates the remainder of the left operand divided by the right operand and assigns the result to the left operand.

```
var num = 5

num += 3 // num is now 8

num -= 2 // num is now 6

num *= 4 // num is now 24

num /= 3 // num is now 8

num %= 5 // num is now 3
```

Comparison Operators

Comparison operators are used to compare values and return a Boolean result (true or false):

• ==: Checks if two values are equal.

• !=: Checks if two values are not equal.

• <: Checks if the left value is less than the right value.

• <=: Checks if the left value is less than or equal to the right value.

• >: Checks if the left value is greater than the right value.

• >=: Checks if the left value is greater than or equal to the right value.

let a = 5

let b = 3

let isEqual = a == b *// false*

let isNotEqual = a != b *// true*

let isLessThan = a < b *// false*

let isGreaterThanEqual = a >= b *// true*

Logical Operators

Logical operators are used to perform logical operations on Boolean values:

- **&&** (Logical AND): Returns true if both operands are true.
- || (Logical OR): Returns true if at least one operand is true.
- **!** (Logical NOT): Inverts the value of a Boolean expression.

let isSunny = **true**

let isWarm = **true**

let isPerfectDay = isSunny && isWarm *// true*

let isGoodWeather = isSunny || isWarm *// true*

let isNotCold = !isWarm *// false*

Ternary Conditional Operator

Swift includes a ternary conditional operator (? :) that allows you to make decisions in a single line of code based on a condition:

```
let number = 7

let isEven = number % 2 == 0 ? "Even" : "Odd"
```

In this example, isEven will be assigned the value "Odd" because 7 is not even.

Conclusion

Operators and expressions are essential components of Swift programming, enabling you to perform a wide range of operations on data. Understanding how to use arithmetic, comparison, logical operators, and compound assignment operators is crucial for building more complex functionality in your iOS applications. In the next sections, we'll explore control flow, functions, and object-oriented programming in Swift.

Section 2.4: Control Flow: Conditionals and Loops

Control flow statements allow you to control the flow of your program's execution. Swift provides several ways to make decisions and repeat tasks using conditionals and loops. In this section, we'll explore conditionals (if, else if, else) and loops (for-in, while, repeat-while) in Swift.

Conditional Statements (if, else if, else)

Conditional statements allow you to execute different blocks of code based on certain conditions. The primary conditional statements in Swift are if, else if, and else.

if Statement

The if statement allows you to execute a block of code if a condition is true:

```
let temperature = 25

if temperature > 30 {

print("It's a hot day!")

}
```

if-else Statement

You can use the if-else statement to provide an alternative code block to execute if the condition is false:

```
let age = 17

if age >= 18 {

print("You can vote.")

} else {

print("You cannot vote.")

}
```

else if Statement

The else if statement allows you to test multiple conditions in sequence:

```
let grade = 85
if grade >= 90 {
print("A")
} else if grade >= 80 {
print("B")
} else if grade >= 70 {
print("C")
} else {
print("F")
}
```

Loops (for-in, while, repeat-while)

Loops are used to execute a block of code repeatedly. Swift provides different types of loops for various use cases.

for-in Loop

The for-in loop is used to iterate over a sequence, such as an array or a range of numbers:

```
let numbers = [1, 2, 3, 4, 5]
```

```
for number in numbers {
print(number)
}
```

while Loop

The while loop continues to execute a block of code as long as a condition remains true:

```
var count = 0
while count < 5 {
print(count)
count += 1
}
```

repeat-while Loop

The repeat-while loop is similar to the do-while loop in other programming languages. It executes a block of code at least once and continues as long as a condition is true:

```
var attempt = 1
repeat {
print("Attempt #\(attempt)")
attempt += 1
} while attempt <= 3
```

Control Transfer Statements (break, continue)

Control transfer statements allow you to change the flow of execution in loops and switch statements. The break statement is used to exit a loop prematurely, and the continue statement is used to skip the rest of the current iteration and move to the next one.

```
let numbers = [1, 2, 3, 4, 5]

for number in numbers {

if number == 3 {

break // Exit the loop when number is 3

}

print(number)

}

for i in 1...5 {

if i % 2 == 0 {

continue // Skip even numbers

}

print(i)

}
```

Conclusion

Control flow statements, including conditionals and loops, are essential for controlling the flow of your Swift programs. They allow you to make decisions based on conditions and repeat tasks efficiently. Understanding how to use if, else if, else, for-in, while, repeat-while, break, and continue statements is vital for building complex and functional iOS applications. In the following sections, we'll delve into functions, object-oriented programming, and more Swift concepts to further enhance your iOS development skills.

Section 2.5: Functions and Methods in Swift

Functions are a fundamental building block of Swift programming. They allow you to encapsulate a piece of code into a reusable and modular unit. In this section, we'll explore how to define, call, and work with functions in Swift.

Defining Functions

In Swift, you can define a function using the func keyword followed by the function name, parameters, return type, and a body enclosed in curly braces. Here's a basic function that adds two numbers:

```
func addNumbers(_ a: Int, _ b: Int) -> Int {

return a + b

}
```

- func: Keyword indicating the start of a function definition.
- addNumbers: Function name.
- (_ a: Int, _ b: Int): Parameters enclosed in parentheses. The underscore _ before parameter names indicates that external parameter names should be omitted when calling the function.

- -> Int: Return type indicating that the function returns an integer.
- { return a + b }: Function body that performs the addition and returns the result.

Calling Functions

Once you've defined a function, you can call it by using its name and providing arguments that match the parameter types. For example:

```
let result = addNumbers(5, 3)

print(result) // Output: 8
```

Function Parameters

Swift allows you to specify external parameter names, which are used when calling the function, and internal parameter names, which are used within the function. In our addNumbers function, we used _ for external parameter names, indicating that callers should omit external names when calling the function. However, you can specify external names explicitly if needed:

```
func divide(_ dividend: Double, by divisor: Double) -> Double {

return dividend / divisor

}

let quotient = divide(10, by: 2)

print(quotient) // Output: 5.0
```

In this example, we've provided explicit external parameter names (dividend and by) to make the function call more descriptive.

Default Parameter Values

Swift allows you to assign default values to function parameters. When a default value is provided, you can omit that parameter when calling the function, and the default value will be used:

```
func greet(name: String, greeting: String = "Hello") {

print("\(greeting), \(name)!")

}

greet(name: "Alice") // Output: Hello, Alice!

greet(name: "Bob", greeting: "Hi") // Output: Hi, Bob!
```

In the greet function, the greeting parameter has a default value of "Hello." If not provided, it will use the default value.

Returning Multiple Values

Swift functions can return tuples to group multiple values together and return them as a single compound value:

```
func getCoordinates() -> (x: Double, y: Double) {

return (3.0, 4.0)

}

let point = getCoordinates()

print("x: \(point.x), y: \(point.y)") // Output: x: 3.0, y: 4.0
```

In this example, the getCoordinates function returns a tuple with two values, representing the x and y coordinates.

Methods

In addition to standalone functions, Swift supports methods, which are functions that are associated with a particular type, such as a class or structure. Methods can be used to perform actions or provide behavior specific to an instance of that type. We'll explore methods in more detail when we cover object-oriented programming in Swift.

Conclusion

Functions are a crucial part of Swift programming, allowing you to encapsulate logic into reusable blocks of code. Understanding how to define functions, work with parameters, provide default values, return values, and use tuples for multiple returns is essential for building modular and maintainable iOS applications. In the upcoming chapters, we'll delve into more advanced Swift concepts and explore object-oriented programming and app development in greater detail.

Chapter 3: Object-Oriented Programming in Swift

Section 3.1: Classes and Objects

Object-oriented programming (OOP) is a programming paradigm that allows you to structure your code around objects, which represent real-world entities or concepts. In Swift, classes and objects are fundamental to OOP. In this section, we'll explore how to define classes, create objects, and work with properties and methods.

Defining Classes

A class is a blueprint or template for creating objects. It defines the structure and behavior of objects of that type. To define a class in Swift, use the class keyword, followed by the class name and a pair of curly braces:

```
class Person {

var name: String = ""

var age: Int = 0

}
```

In this example, we've defined a Person class with two properties: name and age.

Creating Objects (Instances)

Once you've defined a class, you can create objects (also known as instances) of that class. To create an object, use the class name followed by parentheses:

```
let person1 = Person()

let person2 = Person()
```

Here, person1 and person2 are instances of the Person class.

Accessing Properties

You can access the properties of an object using dot notation:

```
person1.name = "Alice"

person1.age = 30

person2.name = "Bob"

person2.age = 25

print("\(person1.name) is \(person1.age) years old.")

print("\(person2.name) is \(person2.age) years old.")
```

This code sets the name and age properties of person1 and person2 and then prints their information.

Methods

Methods are functions defined within a class, allowing you to encapsulate behavior related to the class. Here's how to define a method within a class:

```
class Dog {

var name: String = ""

var breed: String = ""

func bark() {
```

```
print("Woof! Woof!")
}
}
```

In this example, the Dog class has a bark method that prints a dog's bark.

Creating and Using Objects with Methods

You can create objects of a class and invoke their methods:

```
let dog1 = Dog()
let dog2 = Dog()
dog1.name = "Rex"
dog1.breed = "Labrador"
dog2.name = "Buddy"
dog2.breed = "Golden Retriever"
dog1.bark() // Output: Woof! Woof!
dog2.bark() // Output: Woof! Woof!
```

Here, we've created dog1 and dog2 instances and called the bark method on each.

Initialization

Swift classes can have initializers, special methods used for setting up an instance's initial state. For example:

```
class Book {
```

```
var title: String
var author: String
init(title: String, author: String) {
self.title = title
self.author = author
}
}
```

In this Book class, the init method is an initializer that sets the title and author properties when an instance is created.

Conclusion

Classes and objects are fundamental to object-oriented programming in Swift. Classes define the structure and behavior of objects, while objects are instances of classes that hold data and have methods. Understanding how to define classes, create objects, access properties, define methods, and use initializers is essential for building organized and modular iOS applications. In the following sections, we'll delve deeper into OOP concepts like inheritance, encapsulation, and polymorphism in Swift.

Section 3.2: Properties and Methods

In object-oriented programming (OOP), classes encapsulate data and behavior into objects. Properties and methods are the building blocks of classes, allowing you to define the data an object holds and the actions it can perform. In this section, we'll delve into properties and methods in Swift.

Properties

Properties are variables or constants that belong to a class or structure. They define the characteristics or attributes of objects created from that class. In Swift, properties can be stored properties or computed properties.

Stored Properties

Stored properties store values directly. They are associated with an instance of a class or structure. Here's an example:

```
class Rectangle {

var width: Double

var height: Double

init(width: Double, height: Double) {

self.width = width

self.height = height

}

}
```

In this Rectangle class, width and height are stored properties that store the dimensions of a rectangle.

Computed Properties

Computed properties don't store values but provide a getter and an optional setter to compute a value when accessed. Here's an example:

```
class Circle {

var radius: Double

var area: Double {

return Double.pi * radius * radius

}

init(radius: Double) {

self.radius = radius

}

}
```

In the Circle class, area is a computed property that calculates the area of the circle based on the radius property.

Methods

Methods are functions defined within a class or structure. They define the actions that objects of that type can perform. Methods can be instance methods or type methods (static methods).

Instance Methods

Instance methods are associated with an instance of a class or structure and can access and modify the instance's properties. Here's an example:

```
class Counter {

var count = 0
```

```
func increment() {

count += 1

}

func reset() {

count = 0

}

}
```

In the Counter class, increment and reset are instance methods that modify the count property.

Type Methods (Static Methods)

Type methods are associated with the class or structure itself rather than instances. They are prefixed with the static keyword. Here's an example:

```
class MathUtils {

static func square(_ number: Double) -> Double {

return number * number

}

}
```

In the MathUtils class, square is a type method that calculates the square of a number.

Property Observers

Swift provides property observers to observe and respond to changes in property values. You can use willSet to observe before a value changes and didSet to observe after a value changes:

```
class TemperatureConverter {

var celsius: Double = 0.0 {

willSet {

print("Updating celsius from \(celsius)°C to \(newValue)°C")

}

didSet {

print("Updated celsius from \(oldValue)°C to \(celsius)°C")

}

}

}
```

In this example, the celsius property has property observers to log changes.

Conclusion

Properties and methods are essential components of classes and structures in Swift. Properties define the data that objects store, while methods define the actions they can perform. Whether you're working with stored or computed properties, instance or type methods, understanding how to define and use them is crucial for building object-oriented iOS applications. In the following sections, we'll explore more advanced OOP concepts like inheritance, encapsulation, and polymorphism in Swift.

Section 3.3: Inheritance and Polymorphism

Inheritance and polymorphism are core concepts in object-oriented programming (OOP). They allow you to create more complex and organized class hierarchies, enabling code reuse and flexibility. In this section, we'll explore how inheritance and polymorphism work in Swift.

Inheritance

Inheritance is the mechanism by which one class can inherit properties and methods from another class. In Swift, you can create a new class based on an existing class, and the new class is known as a subclass, while the existing class is the superclass.

Here's how you can define a subclass in Swift:

```
class Vehicle {

var speed: Double = 0.0

func accelerate() {

// Accelerate the vehicle

}

}

class Car: Vehicle {

var wheels: Int = 4

}
```

In this example, Car is a subclass of Vehicle. It inherits the speed property and accelerate method from the superclass.

Subclasses can add new properties and methods or override the ones inherited from the superclass. For example, the Car class adds a wheels property specific to cars.

Polymorphism

Polymorphism allows objects of different classes to be treated as objects of a common superclass. It enables code to work with objects in a more abstract way, making your code more flexible and extensible.

In Swift, polymorphism is achieved through method overriding. Subclasses can provide their own implementation for a method that is already defined in the superclass. When you call that method on an object, the implementation from the subclass is invoked.

```
class Animal {

func makeSound() {

// Default animal sound

}

}

class Dog: Animal {

override func makeSound() {

print("Woof! Woof!")

}
```

```
}

class Cat: Animal {

override func makeSound() {

print("Meow!")

}

}
```

In this example, Dog and Cat are subclasses of Animal. Both Dog and Cat override the makeSound method to provide their specific sound.

Polymorphism allows you to create arrays or collections of objects of different subclasses and call their overridden methods without knowing the specific subclass at compile time:

```
let pets: [Animal] = [Dog(), Cat()]

for pet in pets {

pet.makeSound() // Calls the appropriate sound method

}
```

This code demonstrates polymorphism by calling the makeSound method on an array of Animal objects containing both Dog and Cat instances. The correct makeSound method is invoked for each object, showing the flexibility of polymorphism.

Conclusion

Inheritance and polymorphism are powerful tools in Swift's object-oriented programming. They allow you to create hierarchical class structures and write more flexible code that can work with objects of different subclasses in a unified way. Understanding how to define subclasses, use method overriding, and leverage polymorphism is essential for designing scalable and maintainable iOS applications. In the upcoming sections, we'll delve deeper into concepts like encapsulation, access control, and object-oriented design patterns.

Section 3.4: Encapsulation and Access Control

Encapsulation and access control are essential concepts in object-oriented programming (OOP). They help you control the visibility and accessibility of properties and methods within a class or across different classes. In Swift, you can use access control modifiers to define the level of visibility for your class members.

Encapsulation

Encapsulation is the concept of bundling data (properties) and the methods that operate on that data into a single unit (a class) while hiding the internal details from the outside world. Encapsulation helps in achieving data integrity and code organization.

In Swift, you can encapsulate properties by using private access control:

```
class Person {

private var name: String = ""

private var age: Int = 0

func setInfo(name: String, age: Int) {
```

```
self.name = name
self.age = age
}
func getInfo() -> String {
return "Name: \(name), Age: \(age)"
}
}
```

In this example, the name and age properties are marked as private, which means they can only be accessed from within the Person class. The setInfo and getInfo methods provide controlled access to these properties.

Access Control Modifiers

Swift provides several access control modifiers to specify the visibility and accessibility of class members. These modifiers include:

- private: Limits access to the defining source file.
- fileprivate: Limits access to the defining source file.
- internal: Limits access to the defining module (the default access level).
- public: Allows access from any source file, whether in the same module or a different one.
- open: Allows access from any source file and also permits subclassing and overriding.

Here's an example of access control in Swift:

```
public class PublicClass {
internal var internalProperty: Int = 0
fileprivate var filePrivateProperty: Int = 0
private var privateProperty: Int = 0
public func publicMethod() {
// ...
}
}
```

In this example, PublicClass has properties and methods with different access control levels. The publicMethod is accessible from anywhere, while the properties have varying levels of access control.

Benefits of Encapsulation and Access Control

1. **Data Protection**: Encapsulation ensures that the internal state of a class is protected from unauthorized access or modification, helping maintain data integrity.
2. **Code Organization**: Encapsulation organizes code by grouping related properties and methods together within a class, making the codebase more manageable and understandable.
3. **Flexibility**: Access control allows you to expose only the necessary interface of a class to other parts of your code, providing a clean and controlled way to interact with objects.
4. **Security**: By limiting the visibility of certain properties or

methods, you can reduce the risk of accidental misuse or unintended side effects in your code.

Conclusion

Encapsulation and access control are essential principles of OOP that help you create well-structured and secure Swift code. By carefully defining the access levels of class members, you can ensure that your code is maintainable, safe, and follows best practices. In the following sections, we'll explore more advanced OOP concepts and design patterns in Swift to further enhance your iOS development skills.

Section 3.5: Designing Object-Oriented iOS Apps

Designing object-oriented iOS apps involves applying object-oriented programming (OOP) principles to create well-structured and maintainable software. In this section, we'll explore how to design iOS apps using OOP concepts and best practices.

Model-View-Controller (MVC) Architecture

One of the foundational design patterns in iOS development is the Model-View-Controller (MVC) architecture. It divides an app into three components:

1. **Model**: Represents the app's data and business logic. It encapsulates the data and provides methods to manipulate and access it.
2. **View**: Represents the user interface (UI) elements and their layout. Views are responsible for displaying data to the user and handling user interactions.

3. **Controller**: Acts as an intermediary between the Model and View. It handles user input, updates the Model, and updates the View accordingly. Controllers manage the flow of data and user interactions.

Using MVC helps in separating concerns and making your code more organized and maintainable. Each component has a specific role, which makes it easier to modify or extend the app without affecting the other parts.

Object-Oriented iOS App Design Principles

When designing iOS apps with OOP, consider the following principles:

1. **Single Responsibility Principle (SRP)**: Each class or component should have a single responsibility. This makes it easier to understand, modify, and maintain code.
2. **Open/Closed Principle (OCP)**: Classes should be open for extension but closed for modification. This means you should be able to add new functionality to a class without changing its existing code.
3. **Liskov Substitution Principle (LSP)**: Subclasses should be able to be substituted for their parent classes without affecting the correctness of the program.
4. **Interface Segregation Principle (ISP)**: Clients should not be forced to depend on interfaces they do not use. Keep interfaces small and focused on the needs of the client.
5. **Dependency Inversion Principle (DIP)**: High-level modules should not depend on low-level modules. Both should depend on abstractions. Abstractions should not depend on details; details should depend on abstractions.

Design Patterns

iOS development commonly employs design patterns to solve recurring design problems. Some commonly used patterns include:

- **Delegate Pattern**: Allows one object to delegate tasks or responsibilities to another object. It's often used for handling user interactions and callbacks.

- **Singleton Pattern**: Ensures that a class has only one instance and provides a global point of access to that instance. It's used for managing shared resources or data.

- **Observer Pattern**: Defines a one-to-many relationship between objects. When the state of one object changes, all its dependents (observers) are notified and updated automatically. It's used for handling events and notifications.

- **Factory Pattern**: Provides an interface for creating objects, but the subclass decides which class to instantiate. It's used for creating objects with varying behavior.

Conclusion

Designing object-oriented iOS apps involves applying OOP principles, using the MVC architecture, and leveraging design patterns to create well-structured, maintainable, and scalable applications. By following these principles and patterns, you can develop iOS apps that are easier to understand, extend, and maintain, leading to a more efficient and productive development process. In the following chapters, we'll delve into more advanced iOS development topics, including user interfaces, data persistence, networking, and advanced techniques.

Chapter 4: Building User Interfaces with Interface Builder

Section 4.1: Introduction to Interface Builder

Interface Builder is a visual design tool provided by Xcode, Apple's integrated development environment, for creating user interfaces (UIs) for iOS and macOS apps. In this section, we'll introduce you to Interface Builder and its significance in iOS app development.

What is Interface Builder?

Interface Builder is a part of Xcode that allows you to design the user interface of your iOS app visually, without writing code. It provides a drag-and-drop interface for adding UI elements, arranging them on the screen, and configuring their properties.

Here are some key aspects of Interface Builder:

- **Storyboard**: In Interface Builder, UI layouts are often organized in storyboards, which are visual representations of the screens or view controllers in your app. Storyboards help you define the flow and layout of your app's screens.

- **View Controllers**: You can design the content of each screen (or view) using view controllers. Interface Builder provides a canvas where you can design the layout of a view controller's view.

- **UI Elements**: Interface Builder includes a library of UI elements like buttons, labels, text fields, and more. You can drag these elements onto your view controller's canvas and customize their appearance and behavior.

- **Auto Layout**: Interface Builder integrates with Auto Layout, a system for defining how UI elements adapt to different screen sizes and orientations. Auto Layout ensures that your UI looks good on all iOS devices.

Benefits of Using Interface Builder

Using Interface Builder in your iOS development workflow offers several advantages:

1. **Visual Design**: Interface Builder provides a visual interface that makes it easy to design and arrange UI elements without writing code.
2. **Time Efficiency**: It saves time by allowing you to create and modify UI layouts quickly. You can see the results in real-time as you make changes.
3. **Collaboration**: Interface Builder can be used by designers and developers alike, promoting collaboration between teams.
4. **Storyboard Segues**: You can define navigation and transitions between view controllers using storyboard segues, simplifying the implementation of app navigation.

How to Use Interface Builder

To use Interface Builder effectively, follow these general steps:

1. **Create a New Storyboard**: In Xcode, create a new storyboard file for your app. This storyboard will serve as the canvas for designing your app's UI.
2. **Design Your UI**: Open the storyboard in Interface Builder and start adding view controllers and UI elements to your canvas. Use Auto Layout to define how these elements adapt to different screen sizes.

3. **Customize Properties**: Configure the properties and behavior of UI elements by selecting them and adjusting their attributes in the Inspector panel.
4. **Connect Actions and Outlets**: Define the behavior of UI elements by connecting them to your code using actions and outlets.
5. **Test Your UI**: Use the Interface Builder preview to see how your UI looks on various devices and orientations.
6. **Build and Run**: Once you're satisfied with your UI, build and run your app to see it in action on a simulator or physical device.

Conclusion

Interface Builder is a powerful tool for designing user interfaces in iOS app development. It allows you to create visually appealing and responsive UI layouts without writing extensive code. In the following sections, we'll dive deeper into using Interface Builder, Auto Layout, and various UI components to build interactive and user-friendly iOS apps.

Section 4.2: Creating User Interface Elements

In Interface Builder, creating user interface elements is a fundamental step in designing your iOS app's user interface. User interface elements, often referred to as UI elements or controls, include buttons, labels, text fields, images, and more. In this section, we'll explore how to create and customize these UI elements using Interface Builder.

Adding UI Elements

To add UI elements to your view controller's canvas in Interface Builder, follow these steps:

1. **Open Your Storyboard**: Open the storyboard file that corresponds to the view controller where you want to add UI elements.
2. **Select a UI Element**: In the Object Library on the right-hand side of the Interface Builder window, you'll find a list of available UI elements. Common elements include "Button," "Label," "Text Field," "Image View," and more.
3. **Drag and Drop**: Click and drag the UI element you want from the Object Library onto your view controller's canvas. You can position it anywhere on the canvas.
4. **Customize Properties**: After adding the UI element, you can customize its properties in the Attributes Inspector on the right-hand side. You can change its text, color, font, alignment, and other attributes to match your app's design.
5. **Arrange and Size**: Use the Interface Builder canvas to arrange and size the UI elements as needed. You can align them, create stacks, or use Auto Layout to ensure they adapt to different screen sizes.

Common UI Elements

Let's briefly explore some of the common UI elements and their usage:

1. Button: Buttons are used for user interaction. They can trigger actions, like submitting a form or navigating to another screen.

2. Label: Labels display static text or content to the user. They are often used for headings, descriptions, or information display.

3. Text Field: Text fields allow users to input text, numbers, or other data. They are commonly used in forms and for text input.

4. Image View: Image views display images within your app. You can use them for logos, icons, or displaying images from a data source.

5. Switch: Switches represent binary choices, like on/off or yes/no options. They are commonly used in settings screens.

6. Slider: Sliders allow users to select a value from a range. They are used for settings or selecting values within a range.

Connecting UI Elements to Code

Once you've added and customized UI elements, you can connect them to your Swift code to handle user interactions or update their properties programmatically. To do this, you'll use outlets and actions:

- **Outlets**: An outlet is a connection from a UI element (e.g., a label or text field) to a property in your Swift code. This allows you to access and modify the UI element's properties.

- **Actions**: An action is a connection from a UI element (e.g., a button) to a method in your Swift code. When the user interacts with the UI element, the associated method is triggered.

To create an outlet or action, control-click (or right-click) on the UI element in Interface Builder and drag the connection to your Swift code file.

```
@IBOutlet weak var titleLabel: UILabel!

@IBAction func buttonTapped(_ sender: UIButton) {

// Handle button tap event here

}
```

Conclusion

Creating and customizing user interface elements in Interface Builder is a crucial step in iOS app development. It allows you to design visually appealing and interactive interfaces that provide a great user experience. By understanding how to add UI elements, customize their properties, and connect them to your Swift code, you can build feature-rich iOS apps with ease. In the next sections, we'll delve deeper into topics like Auto Layout for responsive designs and connecting UI elements to code for user interaction.

Section 4.3: Auto Layout and Constraints

Auto Layout is a fundamental concept in iOS app development that enables your user interface to adapt to different screen sizes and orientations. It's crucial for creating responsive and visually consistent layouts across various iOS devices. In this section, we'll explore Auto Layout and how to use constraints to define your UI's structure and behavior.

What is Auto Layout?

Auto Layout is a constraint-based layout system provided by Apple in iOS development. Instead of defining fixed positions and sizes for UI elements, Auto Layout uses a set of rules or constraints to determine how elements should be positioned and sized relative to each other and the screen.

Key benefits of Auto Layout include:

- **Adaptability**: Your UI adapts automatically to different screen sizes, resolutions, and orientations, including portrait and landscape modes.

- **Localization**: Auto Layout facilitates localization by allowing UI elements to expand or contract to accommodate different languages and text lengths.

- **Dynamic Content**: It handles dynamic content gracefully, ensuring that UI elements adjust when content changes.

Constraints

Constraints are rules that define the layout and behavior of UI elements within a view. Constraints specify attributes like the element's position, size, spacing, and alignment. You create constraints between UI elements and their parent view or other elements.

Here are some common types of constraints:

- **Leading and Trailing Constraints**: Define the horizontal position of an element relative to the edges of its container.

• **Top and Bottom Constraints**: Determine the vertical position of an element relative to the top and bottom edges of its container.

• **Width and Height Constraints**: Set the size of an element.

• **Equal Width and Equal Height Constraints**: Ensure that two elements have the same width or height.

• **Center Horizontally and Center Vertically Constraints**: Center an element horizontally or vertically within its container.

Using Auto Layout in Interface Builder

To use Auto Layout in Interface Builder, follow these steps:

1. **Select an Element**: Click on the UI element you want to apply Auto Layout to.
2. **Add Constraints**: In the Auto Layout toolbar at the bottom of the Interface Builder window, click on the constraint buttons (e.g., "Pin" or "Align") to create constraints. You can also Control-drag from one element to another to create constraints.
3. **Edit Constraints**: Double-click on a constraint to edit its properties, such as constants or priorities. You can also adjust constraints by selecting them and using the Attributes Inspector.
4. **Update Frames**: After adding or editing constraints, update the frames by selecting "Update Frames" from the Resolve Auto Layout Issues button at the bottom right.
5. **Test Different Sizes**: Use the View as Different Devices and View as Different Orientations buttons in Interface

Builder to preview how your layout adapts to different screens and orientations.

Code and Auto Layout

While Interface Builder is a powerful tool for creating constraints visually, you can also define constraints programmatically in Swift code. This allows for dynamic layout changes based on app logic.

```
// Creating a constraint programmatically

let leadingConstraint = view.leadingAnchor.constraint(equalTo: superview.leadingAnchor, constant: 20)

// Activating the constraint

leadingConstraint.isActive = true
```

You can create and activate constraints using Swift code within your view controllers. This is useful for handling complex layouts or responding to runtime conditions.

Conclusion

Auto Layout and constraints are essential components of iOS app development, ensuring that your user interfaces look and work consistently across a wide range of iOS devices. By mastering Auto Layout, you can create responsive, adaptable, and visually pleasing layouts for your apps. In the next sections, we'll continue to explore other aspects of iOS app development, including connecting user interface elements to code and handling user interactions.

Section 4.4: Connecting UI Elements to Code

Connecting user interface (UI) elements to your Swift code is a crucial aspect of iOS app development. It allows you to respond to user interactions, update UI elements programmatically, and make your app interactive. In this section, we'll explore how to connect UI elements created in Interface Builder to your code using outlets and actions.

Outlets and Actions

To interact with UI elements in Swift code, you use two key concepts:

1. **Outlets**: Outlets are connections that allow you to reference and manipulate UI elements from your code. You create an outlet by defining a property in your Swift code and connecting it to a UI element in Interface Builder.
2. **Actions**: Actions are methods in your Swift code that respond to user interactions with UI elements, such as button taps. You create an action by defining a method in your code and connecting it to a UI element's event, like a button's touch-up-inside event.

Creating Outlets

To create an outlet, follow these steps:

1. Open your storyboard or XIB file in Interface Builder.
2. Select the UI element you want to connect to your code.
3. Open the "Assistant Editor" in Xcode by clicking the "Assistant Editor" button in the top-right corner of the Xcode window.

4. Control-drag from the UI element in Interface Builder to your Swift code file in the assistant editor.
5. When you release the Control key, a pop-up will appear, allowing you to name the outlet. Choose an appropriate name for the property.
6. Click "Connect" to create the outlet.

Now, you have a property in your Swift code that references the UI element, and you can access and manipulate it in your code.

@IBOutlet **weak var** titleLabel: UILabel!

Creating Actions

To create an action, follow these steps:

1. Open your storyboard or XIB file in Interface Builder.
2. Select the UI element (e.g., a button) for which you want to trigger an action.
3. Open the "Assistant Editor" in Xcode by clicking the "Assistant Editor" button in the top-right corner of the Xcode window.
4. Control-drag from the UI element in Interface Builder to your Swift code file in the assistant editor.
5. When you release the Control key, a pop-up will appear, allowing you to configure the action. Choose an appropriate name for the method, select the event you want to trigger the action (e.g., "Touch Up Inside" for a button tap), and choose the target, which is usually "Self."
6. Click "Connect" to create the action.

Now, you have a method in your Swift code that gets called when the specified UI element's event occurs.

```
@IBAction func buttonTapped(_ sender: UIButton) {
// Handle button tap event here
}
```

Using Outlets and Actions

Once you've created outlets and actions, you can use them to:

- Update UI element properties (e.g., changing text, images, visibility).
- Respond to user interactions (e.g., handling button taps, text field input).
- Perform data validation and manipulation.
- Implement navigation and screen transitions.

Here's an example of updating a label's text when a button is tapped:

```
@IBOutlet weak var myLabel: UILabel!
@IBAction func buttonTapped(_ sender: UIButton) {
myLabel.text = "Button Tapped!"
}
```

Conclusion

Connecting UI elements to your Swift code using outlets and actions is a fundamental part of iOS app development. It allows you to create interactive and dynamic user interfaces, respond to user input, and make your app come to life. In the next sections, we'll explore more advanced topics, such as handling user input, data persistence, and networking, to build feature-rich iOS applications.

Section 4.5: Designing Responsive Interfaces

Designing responsive user interfaces is a critical aspect of creating iOS apps that work well on various devices and screen sizes. In this section, we'll explore strategies and best practices for designing responsive interfaces that adapt gracefully to different screen sizes and orientations.

Challenges of Screen Size and Orientation

iOS devices come in various sizes, from small iPhones to large iPads. Additionally, users can switch between portrait and landscape orientations. Designing an interface that looks good and functions well in all these scenarios can be challenging.

Common challenges include:

1. **Limited Screen Real Estate**: Smaller screens have less space for content and may require careful layout adjustments to avoid clutter.
2. **Aspect Ratio Changes**: Switching between portrait and landscape orientations changes the screen's aspect ratio, which can affect the layout of UI elements.
3. **Text Size and Readability**: Text and images must remain readable and visually appealing on different screen sizes.

Using Auto Layout

Auto Layout, as mentioned in a previous section, is a key tool for creating responsive interfaces. By defining constraints between UI elements, you ensure that they adapt and reposition themselves based on the available screen space. Here are some tips for using Auto Layout effectively:

- **Use Constraints with Priority**: Assign priorities to constraints to define which ones are more flexible. This allows you to specify which elements should adapt first when screen size changes.

- **Create Size Classes**: Interface Builder supports size classes, which allow you to define different layouts for various device categories (e.g., compact for iPhones, regular for iPads).

- **Test with Different Devices**: Use the Interface Builder's preview feature to test your layout on various devices and orientations to ensure it adapts correctly.

Stack Views

Stack views are a powerful layout tool in Interface Builder that simplify the creation of complex layouts. You can use stack views to group and arrange UI elements horizontally or vertically. Stack views automatically adjust the spacing and alignment of elements based on available space.

Here's how you can use stack views:

1. Embed UI elements in a stack view by selecting them and choosing "Embed In" > "Stack View" from the Editor menu.
2. Customize the stack view's properties, such as axis (horizontal or vertical), alignment, distribution, and spacing.
3. As the screen size changes, the stack view adjusts the layout

of its elements accordingly.

Adaptive Layout

Adaptive layout is a technique that allows you to create different interface variations for different devices, orientations, and size classes. You can specify different layouts, constraints, or even hide/show certain UI elements based on the user's device or screen size.

To implement adaptive layouts:

- Use size classes in Interface Builder to define different layouts for regular and compact width and height.
- Use the traitCollection property in your view controllers to access information about the current environment, such as the device's size class.
- Implement custom logic in your code to adjust the UI elements and constraints based on the traitCollection.

Dynamic Type

Dynamic Type is a system feature that allows users to adjust the text size of the content in your app. To ensure your app is accessible and visually appealing with different text sizes, use Dynamic Type and make sure your UI elements respond appropriately.

You can support Dynamic Type by:

- Using system fonts and adjusting font weights appropriately.
- Allowing text to expand or contract based on the user's text size settings.

Conclusion

Designing responsive interfaces in iOS apps is essential for providing a great user experience across a wide range of devices and screen sizes. By using Auto Layout, stack views, adaptive layout techniques, and considering Dynamic Type, you can create user-friendly interfaces that look and function well in various scenarios. In the following chapters, we'll explore more advanced topics in iOS app development, including data persistence, networking, and advanced user interface components.

Chapter 5: Model-View-Controller (MVC) Architecture

Section 5.1: Understanding MVC in iOS

The Model-View-Controller (MVC) architectural pattern is a fundamental concept in iOS app development. It provides a structured and organized approach to designing and building iOS applications. In this section, we'll delve into the MVC pattern, its components, and how it helps you create maintainable and scalable iOS apps.

What is MVC?

MVC is a design pattern that separates an application into three interconnected components:

1. **Model**: The Model represents the application's data and business logic. It is responsible for managing data, processing it, and enforcing the application's rules. The Model doesn't directly interact with the user interface.
2. **View**: The View is responsible for presenting the Model's data to the user and handling user interface interactions. It displays the information to the user and sends user input back to the Controller.
3. **Controller**: The Controller acts as an intermediary between the Model and View. It receives user input from the View, processes it, interacts with the Model to fetch or update data, and updates the View accordingly. Controllers manage the flow of information between the Model and View.

Benefits of MVC

The MVC pattern offers several advantages in iOS development:

- **Separation of Concerns**: It enforces a clear separation between data management (Model), user interface (View), and user input handling (Controller), making the codebase more modular and maintainable.

- **Reusability**: Components are loosely coupled, which promotes reusability. For example, you can use the same Model with different Views or reuse a Controller in multiple parts of the app.

- **Scalability**: As your app grows, the MVC pattern helps you scale your development efforts by keeping the code organized and manageable.

- **Testability**: The separation of components simplifies unit testing. You can test the Model, View, and Controller independently, ensuring that each part functions correctly.

MVC in iOS

In an iOS context, here's how the MVC pattern is typically applied:

- **Model**: In iOS, the Model represents the data and business logic of your app. It can include data structures, database interactions, network requests, and more. For example, if you're building a to-do list app, the Model might handle tasks, their properties, and storage.

- **View**: Views in iOS are responsible for rendering user interfaces. They include elements like buttons, labels, tables, and more. Views are defined using Interface Builder, Storyboards, or programmatically in code.

- **Controller**: Controllers in iOS manage the interaction between the Model and View. They receive user input from the View, update the Model as needed, and ensure that the View displays the correct data. View Controllers are a common type of Controller in iOS development.

Implementing MVC in iOS

To implement the MVC pattern effectively in iOS:

1. **Create Models**: Define your data structures and business logic in the Model layer. This might include creating Swift classes or structs to represent objects in your app.
2. **Design Views**: Use Interface Builder or write custom code to design the user interface elements (Views) of your app. Ensure that the Views can display data from the Model.
3. **Develop Controllers**: Create View Controllers or custom controllers to manage the flow of data between the Model and View. Handle user interactions, update the Model, and refresh the View as necessary.
4. **Connect Components**: Use outlets and actions to connect UI elements (View) to your View Controllers (Controller) and implement logic to update the Model and refresh the View.

Here's a simple example of how MVC might work in a basic iOS app:

- **Model**: Represents a list of tasks and provides methods to add, delete, or update tasks.

- **View**: Displays the list of tasks in a table view, with each task represented as a cell.
- **Controller**: Manages the table view, receives user input (e.g., task creation or deletion), and updates the Model accordingly.

Conclusion

Understanding the Model-View-Controller (MVC) architectural pattern is crucial for building well-structured and maintainable iOS apps. By separating data management (Model), user interface (View), and user input handling (Controller), you can create apps that are modular, reusable, and easy to test. In the following sections, we'll explore how to implement each MVC component in iOS app development and discuss best practices for building robust applications.

Section 5.2: Implementing Models in Swift

In the Model-View-Controller (MVC) architectural pattern, the Model is responsible for managing the data and business logic of an iOS app. In this section, we'll focus on implementing Models in Swift, which includes defining data structures, managing data, and implementing the necessary logic for your app.

Defining Data Structures

The first step in implementing a Model is defining the data structures that represent the core objects or entities in your app. These data structures are often defined using Swift classes or structs. Let's take an example of a simple to-do list app to understand this:

```
struct Task {
```

```
var title: String

var isCompleted: Bool

}
```

In this example, we've defined a Task struct with properties like title (to store the task's title) and isCompleted (to indicate whether the task is completed or not).

Managing Data

Once you've defined your data structures, you need to manage the data within your Model. This involves tasks such as creating, updating, deleting, and retrieving data. Here's a basic example of managing tasks within a Model:

```
class TaskManager {

var tasks: [Task] = []

// Method to add a new task

func addTask(title: String) {

let newTask = Task(title: title, isCompleted: false)

tasks.append(newTask)

}

// Method to update the completion status of a task

func updateTaskCompletion(index: Int, isCompleted: Bool) {

guard index >= 0, index < tasks.count else { return }

tasks[index].isCompleted = isCompleted
```

```
}

// Method to delete a task

func deleteTask(at index: Int) {

guard index >= 0, index < tasks.count else { return }

tasks.remove(at: index)

}

}
```

In this example, we've created a TaskManager class to manage a collection of tasks. The class includes methods to add, update, and delete tasks.

Encapsulation and Data Validation

Encapsulation is a key principle when implementing Models. It involves encapsulating data and logic within the Model class or struct and exposing a controlled interface for interacting with the data. In Swift, you can use access control modifiers like private and internal to control access to properties and methods.

Additionally, consider adding data validation logic to your Model to ensure data consistency and integrity. For example, you can validate that a task's title is not empty before adding it to the list.

```
class TaskManager {

var tasks: [Task] = []

// Method to add a new task with data validation

func addTask(title: String) {
```

```
guard !title.isEmpty else { return } // Validate title
let newTask = Task(title: title, isCompleted: false)
tasks.append(newTask)
}
}
```

Using Singletons

In some cases, it's useful to create a singleton Model to ensure a single instance of your Model is shared across different parts of your app. A singleton Model can centralize data management and ensure consistency.

```
class AppModel {
static let shared = AppModel()
private init() {} // Make the initializer private to enforce singleton pattern
var taskManager = TaskManager()
// Add other properties and methods as needed
}
```

With this approach, you can access the shared Model instance throughout your app using AppModel.shared.

Conclusion

Implementing Models in Swift is a fundamental aspect of iOS app development. Models are responsible for managing data and business logic, making them a critical part of the Model-View-Controller

(MVC) pattern. By defining data structures, managing data, encapsulating logic, and considering data validation, you can create robust Models that form the foundation of your iOS applications. In the following sections, we'll explore how to implement Views and Controllers in the MVC pattern and discuss best practices for building user interfaces and handling user interactions.

Section 5.3: Building Views and View Controllers

In the Model-View-Controller (MVC) architectural pattern, Views are responsible for presenting the data from the Model to the user and handling user interactions. View Controllers act as intermediaries between the Model and View, managing the flow of data and interactions. In this section, we'll explore building Views and View Controllers in iOS app development.

Creating Views

Views in iOS represent user interface elements, such as buttons, labels, text fields, tables, and more. You can create Views in several ways:

1. **Interface Builder**: You can use Interface Builder, a visual design tool in Xcode, to create Views and arrange them on the screen. Interface Builder allows you to design the user interface visually, making it accessible to designers and developers alike.
2. **Storyboard**: A storyboard is a visual representation of your app's user interface and the flow between different screens. You can define Views and their relationships within storyboards.
3. **Programmatic Creation**: You can create Views entirely in

code using Swift. This approach gives you complete control over the layout and appearance of Views.

Here's an example of creating a simple label View programmatically:

```
import UIKit

class MyViewController: UIViewController {

override func viewDidLoad() {

super.viewDidLoad()

// Create a UILabel

let label = UILabel()

label.text = "Hello, World!"

label.frame = CGRect(x: 50, y: 100, width: 200, height: 30)

// Add the label to the view hierarchy

self.view.addSubview(label)

}

}
```

Designing User Interfaces

When designing user interfaces (UIs), consider the user experience (UX), accessibility, and visual design principles. Here are some tips:

- **UX Design**: Ensure that the UI is intuitive, easy to navigate, and provides a smooth user experience. Consider user flows, navigation patterns, and interactions.

- **Accessibility**: Make your app accessible to all users, including those with disabilities. Use proper labels for UI elements, provide alternative text for images, and support VoiceOver for screen readers.

- **Visual Design**: Pay attention to the visual design of your UI, including color schemes, typography, spacing, and alignment. A visually appealing UI can enhance user engagement.

Implementing View Controllers

View Controllers are responsible for managing the interaction between Views and the Model. They handle user input, update the Model as needed, and ensure that the View displays the correct data. View Controllers are often associated with specific Views or screens in your app.

Here's an example of a simple View Controller:

```
import UIKit

class TaskListViewController: UIViewController {

var taskManager = TaskManager() // Assume a TaskManager instance from the previous section

override func viewDidLoad() {

super.viewDidLoad()

// Configure the View, e.g., set up a table view

}

@IBAction func addButtonTapped(_ sender: UIButton) {
```

```
// Handle button tap, e.g., show a task creation screen

}

// Implement other methods to respond to user interactions and update the UI

}
```

In this example, TaskListViewController manages the interaction for a task list screen. It has an addButtonTapped method to respond to button taps and update the UI.

Connecting Views and View Controllers

To connect Views with View Controllers, you can use outlets and actions. Outlets allow View Controllers to access and manipulate Views, while actions enable Views to trigger methods in View Controllers.

For example, you can create an outlet to connect a label in your View with a View Controller:

```
class MyViewController: UIViewController {

@IBOutlet weak var myLabel: UILabel!

override func viewDidLoad() {

super.viewDidLoad()

myLabel.text = "Hello, World!"

}

}
```

In Interface Builder, you can control-drag from the label to the View Controller code to create the outlet.

Conclusion

Building Views and View Controllers is a crucial part of iOS app development in the Model-View-Controller (MVC) pattern. Views represent the user interface elements, while View Controllers manage user interactions and data flow. By creating user-friendly, accessible, and visually appealing Views and implementing well-structured View Controllers, you can create engaging and responsive iOS apps. In the following sections, we'll dive deeper into connecting Views to Models, handling user input and gestures, and exploring data persistence in iOS apps.

Section 5.4: Connecting Model, View, and Controller

In the Model-View-Controller (MVC) architectural pattern, one of the key principles is the separation of concerns, which means that the Model, View, and Controller should operate independently and communicate effectively. In this section, we'll explore how to connect these three components in iOS app development.

Model-View Relationship

1. **Model to View**: The Model is responsible for providing data to the View. It doesn't directly update the View but instead notifies the View or the Controller when the data changes. This notification can be achieved through mechanisms like delegates, NotificationCenter, or Key-Value Observing (KVO).

– **Delegates**: Delegation is a common way for the Model to communicate with the View or Controller. The View or Controller acts as the delegate for the Model, and the Model calls delegate methods to notify of changes.

– **NotificationCenter**: NotificationCenter allows the Model to post notifications when data changes. Views or Controllers can register as observers and respond to these notifications.

– **KVO**: Key-Value Observing is a mechanism where the Model publishes properties, and Views or Controllers can observe changes to those properties.

1. **View to Controller**: When a user interacts with the View (e.g., taps a button or enters text), the View informs the associated Controller. This communication is typically achieved through actions and outlets.

– **Actions**: Actions are methods in the Controller that get triggered when a specific user action occurs in the View. You connect UI elements (e.g., buttons) to actions in Interface Builder.

– **Outlets**: Outlets allow the Controller to access and manipulate UI elements in the View. They are typically used for labels, text fields, and other UI elements that need to be updated or interacted with programmatically.

1. **Controller to Model**: The Controller is responsible for managing the interaction between the Model and View. When the Controller receives user input or needs to update the Model, it directly interacts with the Model.

– The Controller can call methods on the Model to update data, create new objects, or retrieve information.

Example of Connecting Model, View, and Controller

Let's consider a to-do list app as an example:

- **Model**: Manages a list of tasks (e.g., TaskManager from previous sections).
- **View**: Displays the list of tasks in a table view.
- **Controller**: Manages the table view and handles user interactions.

Here's how the components interact:

- When the app starts, the Controller (TaskListViewController) requests the list of tasks from the Model (TaskManager) and updates the View (table view) to display them.
- When the user taps the "Add" button in the View, the View informs the Controller through an action (e.g., addButtonTapped). The Controller then creates a new task in the Model.
- If a task's completion status changes (e.g., the user marks a task as completed), the View notifies the Controller. The Controller updates the Model, which in turn updates the View.
- If the Model's data changes (e.g., a new task is added), the Model notifies the View, which then refreshes its display.

This separation of responsibilities and clear communication between Model, View, and Controller helps maintain a clean and organized codebase and ensures that changes in one component do not tightly couple with others.

Data Binding in Other Architectural Patterns

It's important to note that while MVC is a widely used architectural pattern, iOS development has seen the adoption of other patterns, such as MVVM (Model-View-ViewModel) and VIPER (View-Interactor-Presenter-Entity-Routing). These patterns have different approaches to connecting and managing components, often leveraging data binding libraries or reactive programming frameworks like Combine and RxSwift.

In MVVM, for example, the ViewModel acts as an intermediary between the Model and View and often uses data binding to automatically update the View when the ViewModel or Model changes. VIPER, on the other hand, separates components further for improved testability and scalability.

The choice of architectural pattern depends on the complexity and requirements of your app and your team's preferences and expertise.

Conclusion

Connecting the Model, View, and Controller is a fundamental aspect of iOS app development in the Model-View-Controller (MVC) pattern. Clear communication between these components ensures that data flows smoothly, user interactions are handled correctly, and changes in one part of the app don't cause unintended side effects in another. As you continue to build your iOS app, consider the appropriate patterns and mechanisms for connecting components and maintaining a well-structured and maintainable codebase. In the next sections, we'll explore more topics related to iOS development, including handling user input and gestures and persisting data.

Section 5.5: Managing Data Flow in MVC

In the Model-View-Controller (MVC) architectural pattern, managing the flow of data between the Model, View, and Controller is critical for building robust and responsive iOS applications. This section focuses on how data flows between these components and how to handle various scenarios effectively.

Model to View

The Model is responsible for holding and managing the data of your application. When the data in the Model changes, it needs a way to inform the View so that the updated information can be displayed to the user. Several mechanisms can facilitate this communication:

1. **Delegates**: Delegation is a common way to notify the View of changes in the Model. The Model defines a delegate protocol, and the View (or Controller) adopts this protocol and sets itself as the delegate of the Model. When the Model's data changes, it calls delegate methods to inform the View, which then updates itself.

```
// Example of a delegate protocol

protocol TaskManagerDelegate: AnyObject {

func tasksDidUpdate()

}

class TaskManager {
```

```
weak var delegate: TaskManagerDelegate?

func updateTask() {

// Update task logic

delegate?.tasksDidUpdate()

}

}
```

1. **NotificationCenter**: NotificationCenter allows the Model to post notifications when data changes. Views (or Controllers) can register as observers to receive these notifications and respond accordingly.

```
// Example of posting a notification in the Model

NotificationCenter.default.post(name: .tasksDidUpdate, object: nil)

// Example of observing the notification in a View (or Controller)

NotificationCenter.default.addObserver(self, selector: #selector(handleTasksUpdate), name: .tasksDidUpdate, object: nil)
```

1. **Key-Value Observing (KVO)**: With KVO, the Model can publish specific properties, and Views (or Controllers) can observe changes to those properties.

```
// Example of using KVO in the Model
```

```
@objc dynamic var taskCount: Int = 0

// Example of observing the property in a View (or Controller)

taskManager.addObserver(self, forKeyPath: #keyPath(TaskManager.taskCount), options: .new, context: nil)
```

View to Controller

When a user interacts with the View, such as tapping buttons or entering text, the View must inform the associated Controller to handle those interactions. This communication is achieved through actions and outlets:

1. **Actions**: Actions are methods in the Controller that get triggered when specific user actions occur in the View. You connect UI elements (e.g., buttons) to actions in Interface Builder.

```
@IBAction func addButtonTapped(_ sender: UIButton)
{

// Handle the button tap

}
```

1. **Outlets**: Outlets allow the Controller to access and manipulate UI elements in the View. Outlets are typically used for labels, text fields, and other UI elements that need to be updated or interacted with programmatically.

```
@IBOutlet weak var titleLabel: UILabel!
```

Controller to Model

The Controller is responsible for managing user interactions and updating the Model accordingly. When the Controller receives user input or needs to change data in the Model, it directly interacts with the Model. Here are some common scenarios:

1. **User Input**: When the user interacts with the View, the Controller processes the input and calls methods on the Model to update data.

```
@IBAction func addButtonTapped(_ sender: UIButton)
{

// Process user input

taskManager.addTask(title: userInputTextField.text)

}
```

1. **View Updates**: The Controller can update the View by requesting data from the Model and configuring the UI elements accordingly.

```
func updateView() {

titleLabel.text = taskManager.currentTaskTitle

}
```

Conclusion

Effective data flow management between the Model, View, and Controller is essential for creating responsive and maintainable iOS applications following the Model-View-Controller (MVC) pattern. Delegates, NotificationCenter, and KVO facilitate communication from the Model to the View, while actions and outlets connect the View to the Controller. The Controller is responsible for handling user interactions and updating the Model as needed. By mastering these data flow mechanisms, you can create iOS apps that provide a seamless user experience while maintaining a clean and organized codebase.

As you continue your journey in iOS development, consider additional architectural patterns and libraries like Combine and SwiftUI, which offer alternative ways to handle data flow and user interface development in iOS applications.

Chapter 6: Handling User Input and Gestures

Section 6.1: Working with Buttons and Labels

In iOS app development, working with buttons and labels is fundamental to creating interactive user interfaces. Buttons allow users to trigger actions, while labels are used to display text or information. This section explores how to work with buttons and labels in your iOS app.

Creating Buttons

Buttons are a common user interface element for triggering actions. You can create buttons programmatically or in Interface Builder. Here's how to create a button programmatically in Swift:

```
import UIKit

class ViewController: UIViewController {

override func viewDidLoad() {

super.viewDidLoad()

// Create a button

let button = UIButton(type: .system)

button.frame = CGRect(x: 50, y: 100, width: 200, height: 40)

button.setTitle("Click Me", for: .normal)

// Add an action to the button
```

```
button.addTarget(self, action: #selector(buttonTapped), for: .touchUpInside)

// Add the button to the view

view.addSubview(button)

}

@objc func buttonTapped() {

// Handle button tap

print("Button tapped!")

}

}
```

In this example, we create a button, set its title, add an action for the touch-up-inside event, and add the button to the view.

Working with Labels

Labels are used to display static or dynamic text in your app. You can create labels programmatically or in Interface Builder. Here's how to create a label programmatically:

```
import UIKit

class ViewController: UIViewController {

override func viewDidLoad() {

super.viewDidLoad()

// Create a label
```

```
let label = UILabel(frame: CGRect(x: 50, y: 150, width: 200, height: 30))

label.text = "Hello, World!"

// Customize label properties

label.textColor = UIColor.blue

label.font = UIFont.systemFont(ofSize: 16)

// Add the label to the view

view.addSubview(label)

}

}
```

In this code, we create a label, set its text, and customize its appearance.

Interface Builder

You can also create buttons and labels in Interface Builder, a visual tool provided by Xcode. Interface Builder allows you to design your user interface by dragging and dropping elements onto your view controller's storyboard.

1. To create a button or label in Interface Builder, open your storyboard file.
2. Drag a "Button" or "Label" from the Object Library onto your view controller.
3. Customize the button or label properties in the Attributes Inspector.
4. Create actions for buttons or outlets for labels by Ctrl-

dragging from the element to your view controller's code.

Working with buttons and labels is essential for creating interactive and informative iOS apps. Whether you choose to create them programmatically or in Interface Builder depends on your project's requirements and your preferred development workflow.

Section 6.2: Handling Text Input and Keyboard

Text input is a common part of many iOS apps, whether it's entering text in a search bar, filling out forms, or chatting in a messaging app. Handling text input and the keyboard is crucial for providing a smooth user experience. In this section, we'll explore how to work with text input fields and manage the keyboard in iOS.

Text Input Fields

To enable text input, you can use text input fields such as UITextField or UITextView.

UITextField

UITextField is a single-line text input field. You can create it programmatically or in Interface Builder. Here's an example of creating a UITextField programmatically:

```
import UIKit

class ViewController: UIViewController, UITextFieldDelegate {

override func viewDidLoad() {

super.viewDidLoad()
```

```
// Create a text field
let textField = UITextField(frame: CGRect(x: 50, y: 100, width: 200, height: 40))
textField.placeholder = "Enter text"
textField.borderStyle = .roundedRect
// Set the delegate to handle text field events
textField.delegate = self
// Add the text field to the view
view.addSubview(textField)
}
// Implement UITextFieldDelegate methods
func textFieldShouldReturn(_ textField: UITextField) -> Bool {
// Hide the keyboard when Return key is pressed
textField.resignFirstResponder()
return true
}
}
```

In this code, we create a UITextField, set a placeholder text, and define the delegate to handle events. The textFieldShouldReturn method is used to hide the keyboard when the Return key is pressed.

UITextView

UITextView is a multi-line text input field. It's suitable for longer text input. Here's an example of creating a UITextView programmatically:

```
import UIKit

class ViewController: UIViewController, UITextViewDelegate {

override func viewDidLoad() {

super.viewDidLoad()

// Create a text view

let textView = UITextView(frame: CGRect(x: 50, y: 100, width: 200, height: 100))

textView.text = "Enter text"

textView.layer.borderWidth = 1

textView.layer.borderColor = UIColor.lightGray.cgColor

// Set the delegate to handle text view events

textView.delegate = self

// Add the text view to the view

view.addSubview(textView)

}

// Implement UITextViewDelegate methods

func textViewDidBeginEditing(_ textView: UITextView) {
```

```
// Handle text view editing events

}

}
```

In this example, we create a UITextView, set its initial text, and define the delegate to handle events. You can further customize the appearance and behavior of text input fields to match your app's requirements.

Managing the Keyboard

When users tap on a text input field, the keyboard appears. It's essential to manage the keyboard to ensure that it doesn't obscure the content, and users can dismiss it when needed.

Dismissing the Keyboard

To dismiss the keyboard, you can use the resignFirstResponder() method on the text input field. For example:

```
func textFieldShouldReturn(_ textField: UITextField) -> Bool {

// Hide the keyboard when Return key is pressed

textField.resignFirstResponder()

return true

}
```

Similarly, for UITextView, you can call resignFirstResponder() to dismiss the keyboard.

Adjusting the View

In some cases, you may need to adjust the view when the keyboard appears to ensure that the focused text input field remains visible. You can do this by modifying the view's frame or using a UIScrollView to scroll the content.

```
@objc func keyboardWillShow(notification: NSNotification) {

if let keyboardSize = (notification.userInfo?[UIResponder.keyboardFrameEndUserInfoKey] as? NSValue)?.cgRectValue {

// Adjust the view to accommodate the keyboard

let contentInsets = UIEdgeInsets(top: 0, left: 0, bottom: keyboardSize.height, right: 0)

scrollView.contentInset = contentInsets

scrollView.scrollIndicatorInsets = contentInsets

}

}

@objc func keyboardWillHide(notification: NSNotification) {

// Reset the view when the keyboard is dismissed

let contentInsets = UIEdgeInsets.zero

scrollView.contentInset = contentInsets

scrollView.scrollIndicatorInsets = contentInsets

}
```

In this example, we adjust the UIScrollView's content insets when the keyboard appears and reset them when the keyboard is dismissed.

Handling text input and the keyboard is a fundamental part of iOS app development. By using UITextField and UITextView and implementing keyboard management, you can create user-friendly interfaces that provide a seamless text input experience.

Section 6.3: Gesture Recognizers and Touch Events

In iOS app development, interacting with the user's touch gestures is vital for creating intuitive and responsive user interfaces. This section explores how to work with gesture recognizers and handle touch events to respond to user interactions effectively.

Gesture Recognizers

Gesture recognizers are objects that detect and respond to user gestures, such as taps, swipes, pinches, and rotations. iOS provides various built-in gesture recognizers, and you can also create custom ones to suit your app's specific needs.

UITapGestureRecognizer

The UITapGestureRecognizer is used to detect taps on a view. You can add it to a view and specify the number of taps required for recognition.

```
import UIKit

class ViewController: UIViewController {
```

```
override func viewDidLoad() {

super.viewDidLoad()

// Create a view to detect taps

let tapView = UIView(frame: CGRect(x: 50, y: 100, width: 200, height: 200))

tapView.backgroundColor = UIColor.lightGray

// Add the view to the main view

view.addSubview(tapView)

// Create a tap gesture recognizer

let tapGesture = UITapGestureRecognizer(target: self, action: #selector(handleTap(_:)))

tapGesture.numberOfTapsRequired = 1 // Change the number of taps as needed

// Add the gesture recognizer to the view

tapView.addGestureRecognizer(tapGesture)

}

@objc func handleTap(_ gesture: UITapGestureRecognizer) {

// Handle tap gesture

let tappedView = gesture.view

print("View tapped!")

}
```

}

In this example, we create a view and add a UITapGestureRecognizer to it. When the user taps on the view, the handleTap method is called, allowing you to respond to the tap event.

UISwipeGestureRecognizer

The UISwipeGestureRecognizer is used to detect swipes in different directions, such as left, right, up, or down.

```
import UIKit

class ViewController: UIViewController {

override func viewDidLoad() {

super.viewDidLoad()

// Create a view to detect swipes

let swipeView = UIView(frame: CGRect(x: 50, y: 100, width: 200, height: 200))

swipeView.backgroundColor = UIColor.lightGray

// Add the view to the main view

view.addSubview(swipeView)

// Create a swipe gesture recognizer

let swipeGesture = UISwipeGestureRecognizer(target: self, action: #selector(handleSwipe(_:)))
```

```
swipeGesture.direction = .right // Change the swipe direction as needed

// Add the gesture recognizer to the view

swipeView.addGestureRecognizer(swipeGesture)

}

@objc func handleSwipe(_ gesture: UISwipeGestureRecognizer) {

// Handle swipe gesture

print("Swipe detected!")

}

}
```

In this example, we create a view and add a UISwipeGestureRecognizer to it, configured to detect right swipes. You can change the direction property to detect swipes in other directions.

Touch Events

In addition to gesture recognizers, you can also handle touch events directly in your custom views or view controllers.

```
import UIKit

class TouchableView: UIView {

override func touchesBegan(_ touches: Set<UITouch>, with event: UIEvent?) {

// Handle touch events when touches begin
```

```
print("Touches began")

}

override func touchesMoved(_ touches: Set<UITouch>, with event: UIEvent?) {

// Handle touch events when touches move

print("Touches moved")

}

override func touchesEnded(_ touches: Set<UITouch>, with event: UIEvent?) {

// Handle touch events when touches end

print("Touches ended")

}

}
```

In this example, we create a custom view TouchableView and override the touchesBegan, touchesMoved, and touchesEnded methods to respond to touch events.

Understanding how to work with gesture recognizers and touch events is crucial for building interactive iOS apps. By detecting and responding to user gestures and touch interactions, you can create engaging and user-friendly experiences.

Section 6.4: Responding to User Interactions

In iOS app development, responding to user interactions is at the core of creating engaging and interactive apps. This section delves into various ways to handle user interactions, from responding to button taps to managing complex interactions involving multiple views.

Button Taps and Actions

Handling button taps is one of the most common interactions in iOS apps. You can respond to button taps by connecting actions to buttons in Interface Builder or by programmatically adding action targets.

Interface Builder

1. In Interface Builder, select the button you want to add an action to.
2. Open the Connections Inspector.
3. Under "Touch Up Inside," drag from the circle next to "Selector" to your view controller to create a connection.
4. Implement the corresponding action method in your view controller.

```
@IBAction func buttonTapped(_ sender: UIButton) {

// Handle button tap

print("Button tapped!")

}
```

Programmatic Approach

To add a button programmatically and respond to its tap event, you can use the following code:

```
import UIKit

class ViewController: UIViewController {

override func viewDidLoad() {

super.viewDidLoad()

// Create a button

let button = UIButton(type: .system)

button.frame = CGRect(x: 50, y: 100, width: 200, height: 40)

button.setTitle("Click Me", for: .normal)

// Add an action to the button

button.addTarget(self, action: #selector(buttonTapped), for: .touchUpInside)

// Add the button to the view

view.addSubview(button)

}

@objc func buttonTapped() {

// Handle button tap

print("Button tapped!")

}

}
```

In this example, we create a button programmatically, set its title, and add a target-action pair to handle the tap event.

Handling User Input

User input can come from various sources, including text fields, gesture recognizers, and more. Handling user input effectively involves validating and processing the input data.

Text Field Input

When users input text into text fields, you often need to validate and process the input. You can use the UITextFieldDelegate methods to handle text field events.

```
class ViewController: UIViewController, UITextFieldDelegate {

override func viewDidLoad() {

super.viewDidLoad()

// Create a text field

let textField = UITextField(frame: CGRect(x: 50, y: 100, width: 200, height: 40))

textField.placeholder = "Enter text"

textField.borderStyle = .roundedRect

// Set the delegate to handle text field events

textField.delegate = self

// Add the text field to the view

view.addSubview(textField)

}

// Implement UITextFieldDelegate methods
```

```
func textFieldShouldReturn(_ textField: UITextField) -> Bool {

// Hide the keyboard when Return key is pressed

textField.resignFirstResponder()

// Process the text input

if let text = textField.text {

print("User input: \(text)")

}

return true

}

}
```

In this example, we validate the input text and process it when the Return key is pressed in the text field.

Gesture Recognizer Actions

Responding to gesture recognizer actions involves implementing methods to handle gestures, such as taps, swipes, and pinches. These actions can range from simple actions like showing an alert to complex interactions like dragging and dropping views.

```
class ViewController: UIViewController {

override func viewDidLoad() {

super.viewDidLoad()

// Create a view to detect taps
```

```
let tapView = UIView(frame: CGRect(x: 50, y: 100, width: 200, height: 200))

tapView.backgroundColor = UIColor.lightGray

// Add the view to the main view

view.addSubview(tapView)

// Create a tap gesture recognizer

let tapGesture = UITapGestureRecognizer(target: self, action: #selector(handleTap(_:)))

tapGesture.numberOfTapsRequired = 1

// Add the gesture recognizer to the view

tapView.addGestureRecognizer(tapGesture)

}

@objc func handleTap(_ gesture: UITapGestureRecognizer) {

// Handle tap gesture

let tappedView = gesture.view

print("View tapped!")

}

}
```

In this code, we create a view that responds to tap gestures by implementing the handleTap method.

Handling user interactions is a crucial part of iOS app development. By effectively responding to button taps, text input, and gestures, you can create apps that are intuitive and provide a seamless user experience.

Section 6.5: Building Interactive iOS Apps

Building interactive iOS apps involves combining various user interface elements, animations, and user interactions to create engaging and responsive experiences. In this section, we'll explore strategies and techniques for enhancing interactivity in your iOS applications.

Combining Elements

One way to make your iOS app interactive is by combining different UI elements and controlling their behavior based on user input. For example, you can use buttons, switches, and sliders to create settings screens where users can customize their app's behavior.

```
import UIKit

class SettingsViewController: UIViewController {

@IBOutlet weak var switchControl: UISwitch!

@IBOutlet weak var sliderControl: UISlider!

override func viewDidLoad() {

super.viewDidLoad()

// Set initial values

switchControl.isOn = UserDefaults.standard.bool(forKey: "SwitchState")
```

```
sliderControl.value = UserDefaults.standard.float(forKey: "SliderValue")

}

@IBAction func switchValueChanged(_ sender: UISwitch) {

// Handle switch value change

UserDefaults.standard.set(sender.isOn, forKey: "SwitchState")

}

@IBAction func sliderValueChanged(_ sender: UISlider) {

// Handle slider value change

UserDefaults.standard.set(sender.value, forKey: "SliderValue")

}

}
```

In this example, we have a SettingsViewController with a switch and a slider. We store and retrieve the switch state and slider value using UserDefaults.

Animations

Adding animations to your app can significantly enhance interactivity. You can animate the transition between view controllers, create smooth transitions for UI elements, or add subtle visual effects.

```
import UIKit

class AnimatedViewController: UIViewController {
```

```
@IBOutlet weak var animatedView: UIView!

override func viewDidAppear(_ animated: Bool) {

super.viewDidAppear(animated)

// Animate the view's alpha (opacity)

UIView.animate(withDuration: 0.5) {

self.animatedView.alpha = 1.0

}

}

}
```

In this code, we use UIView's animate(withDuration:animations:) method to smoothly fade in a view when the view controller appears.

Gestures and Touch Interactions

Implementing gestures and touch interactions can make your app feel more natural and user-friendly. You can use gesture recognizers to respond to swipe gestures, pinches, and more.

```
import UIKit

class SwipeViewController: UIViewController {

@IBOutlet weak var swipeView: UIView!

override func viewDidLoad() {

super.viewDidLoad()

// Add a swipe gesture recognizer
```

```
let swipeGesture = UISwipeGestureRecognizer(target: self, action: #selector(handleSwipe(_:)))

swipeGesture.direction = .right

swipeView.addGestureRecognizer(swipeGesture)

}

@objc func handleSwipe(_ gesture: UISwipeGestureRecognizer) {

// Handle swipe gesture

if gesture.direction == .right {

// Perform an action, e.g., navigate to the previous screen

navigationController?.popViewController(animated: true)

}

}

}
```

In this example, we add a swipe gesture recognizer to a view, allowing users to swipe right to navigate to the previous screen.

User Feedback and Notifications

Providing feedback to users is essential for interactive apps. You can use UIAlerts to inform users about important actions or errors and use notifications to keep users updated.

```
import UIKit

class FeedbackViewController: UIViewController {

@IBAction func showAlert(_ sender: UIButton) {
```

```
let alertController = UIAlertController(title: "Alert", message: "This is an alert!", preferredStyle: .alert)

let okAction = UIAlertAction(title: "OK", style: .default, handler: nil)

alertController.addAction(okAction)

present(alertController, animated: true, completion: nil)

}

}
```

In this code, tapping a button triggers the display of an alert to provide feedback to the user.

By combining elements, animations, gestures, and user feedback, you can create highly interactive iOS apps that engage and delight users, making their experience more enjoyable and productive.

Chapter 7: Data Persistence in iOS

Section 7.1: Storing Data with UserDefaults

Data persistence is a fundamental aspect of many iOS applications. It involves storing and retrieving data, such as user preferences and small amounts of application-specific data, even after the app is closed and reopened. One commonly used method for simple data storage in iOS is UserDefaults.

What is UserDefaults?

UserDefaults is a lightweight data persistence mechanism provided by Apple's Foundation framework. It allows you to store key-value pairs, where both the keys and values are of certain predefined data types like Int, Float, Double, Bool, URL, Data, and String. UserDefaults is ideal for storing small amounts of data, such as user settings and preferences, that need to be quickly accessed and modified.

Storing Data

To store data using UserDefaults, you need to create an instance of UserDefaults, access its standard instance, and then use the appropriate methods to set values for specific keys.

```
// Storing an Integer

UserDefaults.standard.set(42, forKey: "userScore")

// Storing a String

UserDefaults.standard.set("John Doe", forKey: "userName")

// Storing a Boolean
```

```
UserDefaults.standard.set(true, forKey: "isUserLoggedIn")

// Storing a URL

if let url = URL(string: "https://example.com") {

UserDefaults.standard.set(url, forKey: "websiteURL")

}
```

In this example, we set various types of data using UserDefaults, associating each piece of data with a unique key.

Retrieving Data

Retrieving data from UserDefaults is straightforward. You use the same keys that you used to store the data to retrieve it.

```
if let userScore = UserDefaults.standard.value(forKey: "userScore") as? Int {

print("User Score: \(userScore)")

}

if let userName = UserDefaults.standard.string(forKey: "userName") {

print("User Name: \(userName)")

}

if UserDefaults.standard.bool(forKey: "isUserLoggedIn") {

print("User is logged in.")

}
```

```
if let websiteURL = UserDefaults.standard.url(forKey: "websiteURL") {

print("Website URL: \(websiteURL)")

}
```

Here, we retrieve the previously stored data from UserDefaults and print it. Note that we use optional binding (if let) to safely unwrap the retrieved values.

UserDefaults Synchronization

UserDefaults provides methods for data synchronization. By default, changes made to UserDefaults are not immediately saved to disk, but they are cached in memory. You can use the synchronize() method to force UserDefaults to write changes to disk immediately.

```
UserDefaults.standard.synchronize()
```

However, starting with iOS 8.0 and macOS 10.9, calling synchronize() is generally unnecessary because UserDefaults automatically synchronizes changes to disk at appropriate times.

UserDefaults is a simple and convenient way to store and retrieve user-specific data and preferences in your iOS applications. It's best suited for small amounts of data, and for more complex data storage needs, you might consider using other solutions like Core Data or file storage.

Section 7.2: Working with Files and Directories

While UserDefaults is suitable for storing small amounts of data, iOS provides other mechanisms for handling more extensive and structured data storage. This section explores working with files and directories in iOS, allowing you to manage data like documents, images, and other user-generated content.

File System Basics

In iOS, each app runs in its own sandboxed environment, which includes a private file system. This sandboxed file system ensures that apps cannot access the files of other apps, providing data security and isolation.

Accessing the App's Documents Directory

The most common location for storing user-generated content is the app's Documents directory. You can access this directory using the FileManager class.

```
if let documentsDirectory = FileManager.default.urls(for: .documentDirectory, in: .userDomainMask).first {

print("Documents Directory: \(documentsDirectory)")

}
```

This code snippet retrieves the URL of the app's Documents directory, which is a location where you can save user-generated files like documents and images.

Writing to and Reading from Files

To write data to a file, you can use the Data class to represent the content and the FileManager class to save it to a specific location.

```
let fileName = "example.txt"

let fileContent = "Hello, iOS File System!"
```

```
if let documentsDirectory = FileManager.default.urls(for: .documentDirectory, in: .userDomainMask).first {
let fileURL = documentsDirectory.appendingPathComponent(fileName)
do {
try fileContent.write(to: fileURL, atomically: false, encoding: .utf8)
print("File saved at: \(fileURL.path)")
} catch {
print("Error writing to file: \(error.localizedDescription)")
}
}
```

In this example, we create a text file named "example.txt" in the Documents directory and write the content "Hello, iOS File System!" to it.

To read from a file, you can use the String constructor or the Data class to retrieve the content.

```
let fileName = "example.txt"
if let documentsDirectory = FileManager.default.urls(for: .documentDirectory, in: .userDomainMask).first {
let fileURL = documentsDirectory.appendingPathComponent(fileName)
do {
let fileContent = try String(contentsOf: fileURL, encoding: .utf8)
```

```
print("File content: \(fileContent)")

} catch {

print("Error reading from file: \(error.localizedDescription)")

}

}
```

In this code, we read the content of the “example.txt” file we previously created.

Deleting and Managing Files

You can delete files using the FileManager class by specifying the file’s URL.

```
let fileName = "example.txt"

if let documentsDirectory = FileManager.default.urls(for: .documentDirectory, in: .userDomainMask).first {

let fileURL = documentsDirectory.appendingPathComponent(fileName)

do {

try FileManager.default.removeItem(at: fileURL)

print("File deleted: \(fileURL.path)")

} catch {

print("Error deleting file: \(error.localizedDescription)")

}

}
```

Here, we delete the "example.txt" file.

Managing files also involves checking for their existence, copying, and moving them, all of which can be accomplished using the FileManager class.

Working with files and directories allows your iOS app to handle various types of data, from user-generated content to documents and configurations. Understanding the iOS file system and its APIs is essential for effective data management within your app.

Section 7.3: Using Core Data for Data Storage

Core Data is a powerful and flexible framework provided by Apple for data storage and management in iOS applications. It's particularly well-suited for complex data models and relational databases. In this section, we'll explore how to use Core Data for data persistence in your iOS app.

Introduction to Core Data

Core Data is an object graph and persistence framework that allows you to work with data in a high-level, object-oriented manner. It abstracts the underlying SQLite database, making it easier to work with data models, relationships, and queries.

Setting Up a Core Data Stack

Before you can use Core Data, you need to set up a Core Data stack, which includes:

1. **Managed Object Model**: Defines the structure of your data model, including entities, attributes, and relationships.

You can create this using the Xcode data model editor.

2. **Managed Object Context**: Represents a scratchpad for working with data. You typically have a main context for the main thread and background contexts for background tasks.
3. **Persistent Store Coordinator**: Manages the interaction between the data in your app and the persistent store (SQLite database by default).
4. **Persistent Store**: The physical storage for your data, such as an SQLite database file.

Defining a Data Model

You define your data model using the Core Data data model editor in Xcode. You create entities to represent objects in your app, attributes to define their properties, and relationships to establish connections between them.

Here's an example of defining a simple data model for a "Task" entity with attributes "title" and "dueDate":

```
import CoreData

@objc(Task)

public class Task: NSManagedObject {

@NSManaged public var title: String?

@NSManaged public var dueDate: Date?

}
```

Fetching and Saving Data

To fetch data from Core Data, you use a NSFetchRequest to define the criteria for your query. For example, to fetch all tasks:

```
let fetchRequest: NSFetchRequest<Task> = Task.fetchRequest()

do {

let tasks = try context.fetch(fetchRequest)

for task in tasks {

print("Task Title: \(task.title ?? "N/A"), Due Date: \(task.dueDate ?? Date())")

}

} catch {

print("Error fetching tasks: \(error.localizedDescription)")

}
```

To save data, you create a new managed object and add it to the managed object context:

```
let newTask = Task(context: context)

newTask.title = "Complete Core Data section"

newTask.dueDate = Date()

do {

try context.save()

} catch {
```

```
print("Error saving task: \(error.localizedDescription)")
}
```

Relationships and Fetching Related Data

Core Data supports relationships between entities. For example, you can have a "Category" entity related to the "Task" entity. Fetching related data is straightforward:

```
let categoryFetchRequest: NSFetchRequest<Category> = Category.fetchRequest()

categoryFetchRequest.predicate = NSPredicate(format: "name == %@", "Work")

do {

if let workCategory = try context.fetch(categoryFetchRequest).first {

if let workTasks = workCategory.tasks as? Set<Task> {

for task in workTasks {

print("Task Title: \(task.title ?? "N/A"), Due Date: \(task.dueDate ?? Date())")

}

}

}

} catch {

print("Error fetching tasks in the Work category: \(error.localizedDescription)")
```

}

Core Data provides a robust and efficient way to manage and persist data in your iOS app. It's particularly useful when dealing with complex data structures, relationships, and querying requirements. By using Core Data, you can create scalable and maintainable data-driven apps with ease.

Section 7.4: Networking and Data Retrieval

Networking is a fundamental part of many iOS applications, as it enables data retrieval from remote servers and services. In this section, we'll explore networking in iOS, including making HTTP requests, handling responses, and working with data from external sources.

Introduction to Networking in iOS

iOS provides several ways to perform network requests, but one of the most commonly used methods is through the URLSession framework. URLSession is a powerful and flexible API for making HTTP requests and handling responses.

Making HTTP Requests with URLSession

To make an HTTP GET request using URLSession, you create a URLSessionDataTask and provide it with a URL:

```
let url = URL(string: "https://api.example.com/data")!

let task = URLSession.shared.dataTask(with: url) { data, response, error in

if let error = error {
```

```
print("Error: \(error.localizedDescription)")
return
}
if let data = data {
// Process the data
print("Data received: \(data.count) bytes")
}
}
task.resume()
```

In this code, we initiate an HTTP GET request to "https://api.example.com/data" using a shared URLSession. The completionHandler is called when the request is complete, whether it succeeds or encounters an error.

Parsing JSON Data

When working with web APIs, it's common to receive data in JSON format. You can parse JSON data using the Codable protocol in Swift. Suppose you have a data structure that corresponds to the JSON data:

```
struct Item: Codable {
let id: Int
let name: String
}
```

You can decode the JSON data like this:

```
if let jsonData = data {
do {
let items = try JSONDecoder().decode([Item].self, from: jsonData)
for item in items {
print("Item ID: \(item.id), Name: \(item.name)")
}
} catch {
print("Error decoding JSON: \(error.localizedDescription)")
}
}
```

This code decodes an array of "Item" objects from the received JSON data.

Handling RESTful APIs

RESTful APIs are common in web development, and iOS apps often interact with them. You can use URLSession to make various types of HTTP requests, including GET, POST, PUT, and DELETE, to interact with RESTful APIs.

Advanced Networking Techniques

iOS provides additional features for more advanced networking scenarios. You can implement authentication mechanisms, handle background downloads/uploads, and manage network tasks efficiently.

Networking Best Practices

When working with networking in iOS, it's essential to follow best practices for security, performance, and user experience. Securely handling sensitive data, optimizing network requests, and providing feedback to users are critical considerations.

In conclusion, networking is a crucial aspect of iOS development, enabling your app to interact with external data sources, services, and APIs. URLSession and Codable make it relatively straightforward to perform network requests and process data in a structured way. By understanding networking fundamentals and best practices, you can build robust and efficient network-connected iOS apps.

Section 7.5: Best Practices for Data Persistence

Data persistence is a critical aspect of iOS app development, ensuring that user data is securely stored and accessible across app sessions. In this section, we'll delve into best practices for data persistence in iOS, covering aspects such as data security, performance, and user experience.

Data Encryption and Security

When dealing with sensitive user data, such as login credentials or personal information, it's essential to prioritize data security. iOS provides built-in mechanisms for data encryption and secure storage.

- **Keychain Services**: For storing sensitive information like passwords, use the Keychain Services API. The Keychain securely stores data in an encrypted format, making it difficult for unauthorized access.

```
import Security

let keychainItem = KeychainPasswordItem(service: "MyApp", account: "user@example.com")

do {

try keychainItem.savePassword("superSecretPassword")

} catch {

print("Error saving password: \(error.localizedDescription)")

}
```

- **Data Protection**: iOS offers data protection classes that automatically encrypt data stored in the app's file system. You can specify the appropriate data protection class when creating or saving files.

Data Caching and Performance

Efficiently managing cached data can significantly impact your app's performance and user experience. Here are some caching best practices:

- **Cache Invalidation**: Implement a strategy for cache invalidation. Determine when cached data should expire or become invalid, and update it accordingly. Use mechanisms like time-based expiration or versioning.

- **Use Disk Caching**: For large or frequently accessed data, consider caching it to the device's file system. Disk caching can improve app performance by reducing the need to re-download data.

Offline Access and Syncing

Many apps need to support offline access and data synchronization. To provide a seamless experience, consider these practices:

- **Local Database**: Use Core Data or a local database to store essential data that should be available offline. This allows users to access critical content even when not connected to the internet.

- **Syncing Mechanism**: Implement a robust syncing mechanism that can update local data when the app is online. Ensure that conflicts are handled gracefully, and users are informed of the sync status.

User Experience and Feedback

Data persistence is often transparent to users, but it can significantly affect their experience. Consider these aspects for a better user experience:

- **Progress Indicators**: When performing data operations like saving or syncing, provide clear progress indicators or feedback to users. This keeps them informed about ongoing tasks.

- **Data Recovery**: Implement data recovery mechanisms in case of app crashes or unexpected errors. Users should not lose their data due to app instability.

- **Privacy and Consent**: Always respect user privacy and seek their consent when storing or processing personal data. Clearly communicate your app's data handling practices in the privacy policy.

Testing and Quality Assurance

Thoroughly test data persistence features in your app to ensure reliability and robustness. Consider the following testing strategies:

- **Unit Testing**: Write unit tests to verify the correctness of data storage and retrieval operations.

- **Integration Testing**: Conduct integration tests to ensure that data persistence works correctly in the context of your app's workflows.

- **Edge Cases**: Test edge cases, such as low storage space or interrupted network connections, to verify that your app behaves gracefully.

By adhering to best practices for data persistence in iOS, you can create apps that offer a secure, responsive, and user-friendly experience. Data security, efficient caching, and thoughtful user feedback contribute to the overall quality of your app and user satisfaction.

Chapter 8: Networking and API Integration

Section 8.1: Introduction to Networking in iOS

Networking is a fundamental aspect of iOS app development, allowing your app to communicate with remote servers and services. Whether you're fetching data from a web API, uploading user-generated content, or supporting real-time features, understanding how networking works in iOS is crucial.

Networking Basics

At its core, networking involves sending and receiving data over a network, usually the internet. In iOS, you use the URLSession framework to manage network tasks. URLSession provides a set of APIs for making HTTP requests, handling responses, and managing data transfer.

URLSession

URLSession is a versatile API that allows you to perform various network-related tasks, including:

- **Making HTTP requests**: You can create URLSessionDataTask objects to send GET, POST, PUT, or DELETE requests to remote servers.

- **Downloading and uploading data**: URLSessionDownloadTask and URLSessionUploadTask enable you to download files or upload data to and from remote servers.

- **Handling background tasks**: URLSession supports background tasks, allowing your app to continue network operations even when it's not in the foreground.

Asynchronous Networking

Networking in iOS is inherently asynchronous. This means that when you make a network request, your app doesn't wait for the response. Instead, it continues executing other tasks, and the network response is processed in the background.

To handle asynchronous operations, URLSession uses completion handlers. A completion handler is a block of code that gets executed when a task, such as a data task or download task, is completed. This asynchronous nature ensures that your app remains responsive while waiting for network responses.

Error Handling

Networking operations can encounter errors, such as network connectivity issues or server failures. It's essential to implement robust error handling in your networking code to provide a good user experience.

URLSession provides error objects that contain information about what went wrong during a network task. By examining these errors, you can take appropriate actions, such as displaying error messages or retrying the operation.

Security and Authentication

Security is a paramount concern when dealing with networking. iOS provides mechanisms to ensure secure communication with remote servers. These mechanisms include:

- **HTTPS**: Always use HTTPS for secure data transmission. iOS enforces secure connections and doesn't allow unsecured HTTP connections by default.

- **SSL Pinning**: You can implement SSL pinning to verify the server's certificate, ensuring that your app communicates only with trusted servers.

- **Authentication**: iOS supports various authentication methods, such as OAuth, API keys, and token-based authentication, to secure access to APIs and services.

In conclusion, networking is a critical part of iOS app development, enabling your app to connect with external resources. URLSession is a powerful framework for managing network tasks, and understanding its asynchronous nature and error handling is essential. Additionally, prioritizing security and authentication ensures that your app communicates securely with remote servers. In the following sections, we'll delve deeper into various networking topics, including making HTTP requests, parsing data, and handling advanced networking scenarios.

Section 8.2: Making HTTP Requests with URLSession

In iOS development, making HTTP requests is a fundamental task when your app needs to interact with web services, APIs, or retrieve data from remote servers. URLSession is a powerful framework for managing these network requests.

Creating a URLSession

To start making HTTP requests, you'll typically use an instance of URLSession. URLSession provides a range of configuration options to tailor your requests to specific needs. Here's how you can create a default URLSession:

```
let session = URLSession.shared
```

Alternatively, you can create a custom URLSession with your configuration:

```
let configuration = URLSessionConfiguration.default

let session = URLSession(configuration: configuration)
```

Making a GET Request

The most common type of HTTP request is a GET request, used for retrieving data from a server. To make a GET request, you create a URLSessionDataTask and specify the URL:

```
if let url = URL(string: "https://api.example.com/data") {

let task = session.dataTask(with: url) { data, response, error in

if let error = error {

print("Error: \(error.localizedDescription)")

return

}

if let data = data {

// Process the data

print("Data received: \(data.count) bytes")

}

}
```

```
task.resume()

}
```

In this example, a dataTask is created, which sends a GET request to "https://api.example.com/data." The completion handler is called when the request is complete, allowing you to handle the response or any errors.

Making Other Types of Requests

URLSession supports various HTTP request methods, including POST, PUT, and DELETE. To make a request with a different HTTP method, you can specify it in the URLRequest:

```
if let url = URL(string: "https://api.example.com/update") {

var request = URLRequest(url: url)

request.httpMethod = "POST" // Change to the desired HTTP method

// Set request body data if needed

// request.httpBody = ...

let task = session.dataTask(with: request) { data, response, error in

// Handle the response or error

}

task.resume()

}
```

Handling Responses

The completion handler for a URLSessionDataTask provides access to the data received from the server, the HTTP response, and any errors. You can parse the data, extract headers, and check the HTTP status code to handle the response appropriately.

Error Handling

Networking operations can encounter errors, such as network connectivity issues or server problems. It's essential to implement error handling to provide a good user experience. In the completion handler, you should check for and handle errors, such as:

```
if let error = error {

print("Error: \(error.localizedDescription)")

// Handle the error, e.g., display an error message to the user

return

}
```

By implementing proper error handling, you can gracefully manage unexpected situations and provide feedback to users when network requests fail.

Background Downloads and Uploads

URLSession also supports background downloads and uploads, allowing your app to continue networking tasks even when it's in the background or not actively running. This is useful for scenarios like downloading large files or syncing data.

In conclusion, URLSession is a robust framework for making HTTP requests in iOS. It offers flexibility, error handling, and support for various HTTP methods. Understanding how to create sessions, make requests, and handle responses is essential for building apps that interact with remote servers and services. In the next sections, we'll explore topics like parsing JSON data, handling RESTful APIs, and advanced networking techniques.

Section 8.3: Parsing JSON Data

In iOS app development, working with web APIs often involves exchanging data in JSON (JavaScript Object Notation) format. JSON is a lightweight data interchange format that's easy to read and write for both humans and machines. When your app makes requests to an API, you'll likely receive JSON data in the response. Parsing this data is a crucial step in extracting meaningful information.

What is JSON?

JSON is a text-based data format consisting of key-value pairs. It is commonly used for transmitting data between a server and a client. Here's a simple JSON example:

```
{
"name": "John Doe",
"age": 30,
"email": "john@example.com"
}
```

In this JSON object, there are three key-value pairs: "name," "age," and "email."

Parsing JSON in Swift

Swift provides built-in support for parsing JSON data using the JSONSerialization class. You can convert JSON data received from a network request into native Swift data types such as dictionaries and arrays. Here's a basic example of parsing JSON:

```
if let jsonData = jsonString.data(using: .utf8) {

do {

if let json = try JSONSerialization.jsonObject(with: jsonData, options: []) as? [String: Any] {

// Access JSON data here

if let name = json["name"] as? String {

print("Name: \(name)")

}

if let age = json["age"] as? Int {

print("Age: \(age)")

}

}

} catch {

print("Error parsing JSON: \(error.localizedDescription)")

}
```

```
}
```

In this example, we first convert a JSON-formatted string (jsonString) into a Data object. Then, we use JSONSerialization to parse the JSON data into a Swift dictionary. Finally, we access specific values from the dictionary.

Codable Protocol

Swift introduced the Codable protocol to simplify the process of encoding and decoding JSON data. By adopting Codable, your custom data types can be automatically converted to and from JSON. This approach is particularly useful when working with complex data structures.

Here's an example of a Codable data model:

```
struct Person: Codable {

let name: String

let age: Int

let email: String

}
```

You can use the JSONDecoder and JSONEncoder classes to decode JSON data into Swift objects and encode Swift objects into JSON, respectively.

Handling Nested JSON

JSON data often includes nested structures, such as arrays of objects. Parsing nested JSON involves navigating through the hierarchy to access the desired data. Swift's Codable protocol simplifies this process by automatically handling nested structures.

Error Handling

When parsing JSON, it's essential to account for potential errors, such as malformed JSON or data that doesn't match the expected format. The try-catch block in Swift allows you to catch and handle parsing errors gracefully.

In summary, parsing JSON data is a common task in iOS app development, especially when working with web APIs. Swift provides powerful tools like JSONSerialization and the Codable protocol to make JSON parsing efficient and straightforward. Proper error handling ensures that your app can handle unexpected data gracefully. In the next sections, we'll explore more advanced networking topics, including handling RESTful APIs and performing advanced networking techniques.

Section 8.4: Handling RESTful APIs

REST (Representational State Transfer) is an architectural style for designing networked applications. RESTful APIs (Application Programming Interfaces) follow REST principles and are widely used for web services. When working with RESTful APIs in iOS development, you interact with endpoints to perform actions like retrieving data, creating resources, updating resources, and deleting resources. This section covers essential concepts and techniques for handling RESTful APIs in your iOS app.

HTTP Methods

RESTful APIs use HTTP methods to specify the desired action. The most common HTTP methods are:

- **GET:** Used for retrieving data from the server.
- **POST:** Used for creating new resources on the server.
- **PUT:** Used for updating existing resources on the server.
- **DELETE:** Used for deleting resources on the server.

RESTful Endpoints

Each RESTful API endpoint represents a specific resource or collection of resources. Endpoints are identified by URLs and are associated with one or more HTTP methods. For example:

- GET /api/posts: Retrieves a list of posts.
- GET /api/posts/123: Retrieves a specific post.
- POST /api/posts: Creates a new post.
- PUT /api/posts/123: Updates an existing post.
- DELETE /api/posts/123: Deletes a post.

Authentication

Many RESTful APIs require authentication to access protected resources. Common authentication methods include API keys, OAuth tokens, or username/password combinations. You need to include authentication credentials in your requests' headers or body, depending on the API's requirements.

Handling Responses

When making requests to a RESTful API, you'll receive responses in various formats, commonly JSON or XML. You'll need to parse these responses, as discussed in the previous section, to extract relevant data for your app.

Libraries and Tools

iOS provides URLSession for making HTTP requests, but you may also use third-party libraries like Alamofire to simplify network code. Alamofire abstracts some of the complexities of URLSession, making it more convenient for handling RESTful APIs.

API Documentation

When working with a RESTful API, refer to its documentation. API documentation provides essential information about available endpoints, required authentication, request and response formats, and example usage. Understanding the API documentation is crucial for integrating the API effectively into your app.

Error Handling

Handling errors gracefully is vital when working with RESTful APIs. APIs may return various HTTP status codes (e.g., 200 for success, 400 for bad request, 401 for unauthorized, 404 for not found, 500 for server error). You should check the status code in the response and handle errors accordingly in your app.

Here's an example of error handling using URLSession:

```
let task = session.dataTask(with: url) { data, response, error in

if let error = error {

print("Error: \(error.localizedDescription)")

// Handle the error, e.g., display an error message to the user
```

```
return
}
guard let httpResponse = response as? HTTPURLResponse else {
print("Invalid response")
return
}
switch httpResponse.statusCode {
case 200:
// Process the successful response
case 400:
// Handle bad request
case 401:
// Handle unauthorized
case 404:
// Handle not found
case 500:
// Handle server error
default:
print("Unhandled status code: \(httpResponse.statusCode)")
}
```

}

In this example, we check the HTTP status code to determine the type of error or success response.

In conclusion, handling RESTful APIs is a fundamental aspect of iOS app development, as it allows your app to interact with web services and retrieve data from remote servers. Understanding HTTP methods, endpoints, authentication, and error handling is crucial for building robust and reliable apps that communicate effectively with APIs. Utilizing libraries like Alamofire and referencing API documentation can simplify the process of integrating RESTful APIs into your iOS app. In the next section, we'll explore advanced networking techniques, including asynchronous programming and concurrency.

Section 8.5: Advanced Networking Techniques

In iOS app development, there are situations where you need to implement advanced networking techniques to optimize performance, responsiveness, and user experience. This section explores some of these techniques and concepts.

Asynchronous Programming

Many networking tasks in iOS should be performed asynchronously to avoid blocking the main thread, which would lead to unresponsive user interfaces. Asynchronous programming allows you to start a task and continue executing other code while waiting for the task to complete. Common mechanisms for achieving asynchronicity include Grand Central Dispatch (GCD) and closures.

Here's an example of making an asynchronous network request using GCD:

```
// Perform the network request asynchronously

DispatchQueue.global().async {

// Make the request and handle the response here

let data = try? Data(contentsOf: url)

DispatchQueue.main.async {

// Update the UI with the response on the main thread

if let data = data {

// Process the data

} else {

// Handle the error

}

}

}
```

Background Fetch and Refresh

To keep your app's content up-to-date even when it's not in the foreground, you can implement background fetch and refresh. This allows your app to periodically fetch new data in the background and update its content. You can configure background fetch in the app's capabilities and schedule the frequency of fetch operations.

Pagination

When dealing with large datasets from a server, pagination is a common technique. Instead of loading all data at once, you fetch a limited portion, display it, and then load more data as the user scrolls or interacts with the app. This approach enhances performance and reduces memory usage.

Caching

Caching involves storing previously fetched data locally on the device to avoid unnecessary network requests. iOS provides various caching mechanisms, including URLCache for HTTP content caching and NSCache for temporary in-memory caching. Caching can significantly improve app performance and reduce data usage.

Rate Limiting

Some APIs impose rate limits on the number of requests you can make within a specific time frame. To stay within these limits, you may need to implement rate limiting in your app. This can be achieved by tracking the rate of requests and ensuring that your app does not exceed the allowed limit.

Resumable Downloads

When downloading large files, it's essential to support resumable downloads. This allows users to pause and resume downloads, ensuring a smooth experience even if the network connection is unreliable or the download is interrupted.

Network Monitoring

Monitoring the network connection is crucial for providing a seamless user experience. You can use Reachability or

NWPathMonitor to check the network status and adapt your app's behavior accordingly. For example, you might display a message to the user when there is no network connection.

Security Considerations

When implementing advanced networking techniques, security should be a top priority. Ensure that you follow best practices for secure communication, such as using HTTPS for all network requests and handling sensitive data securely. Additionally, consider data privacy and user consent when implementing background fetch and refresh.

In summary, advanced networking techniques in iOS development are essential for building responsive and efficient apps that deliver a great user experience. Asynchronous programming, background fetch, pagination, caching, rate limiting, resumable downloads, network monitoring, and security considerations are crucial aspects of implementing advanced networking functionality in your iOS app. By mastering these techniques, you can create robust and reliable networking solutions that meet the needs of your users.

Chapter 9: Building Table Views and Collection Views

Table views and collection views are fundamental components in iOS app development for displaying lists of items or grid-based content. This chapter covers various aspects of creating and customizing table views and collection views to present data efficiently and interactively.

Section 9.1: Creating Table Views

Table views are commonly used to display lists of items, such as contacts, messages, or news articles. In iOS, you typically create table views using UITableView. Here's a step-by-step guide to creating a basic table view:

1. Adding a Table View to the Interface

You can add a table view to your app's interface using Interface Builder or programmatically in code. In Interface Builder, drag and drop a Table View component onto your view controller's scene. Make sure to set constraints to define its position and size.

2. Setting Up Data Source and Delegate

A table view relies on data provided by a data source and responds to user interactions through a delegate. Conform to the UITableViewDataSource and UITableViewDelegate protocols in your view controller:

class MyTableViewController: UIViewController, UITableViewDataSource, UITableViewDelegate {

```
// ...

}
```

3. Creating a Data Source

Define the data source for your table view. This can be an array of items, a dictionary, or any other data structure that represents your data. For example, an array of strings:

```
let items = ["Item 1", "Item 2", "Item 3"]
```

4. Implementing Data Source Methods

The data source methods, such as numberOfSections(in:) and tableView(_:numberOfRowsInSection:), provide information about the structure of the table view and the number of rows in each section:

```
func numberOfSections(in tableView: UITableView) -> Int {

return 1

}

func tableView(_ tableView: UITableView, numberOfRowsInSection section: Int) -> Int {

return items.count

}
```

5. Populating Cells

Implement the tableView(_:cellForRowAt:) method to configure and return a cell for each row:

```
func tableView(_ tableView: UITableView, cellForRowAt indexPath: IndexPath) -> UITableViewCell {

let cell = tableView.dequeueReusableCell(withIdentifier: "MyCellIdentifier", for: indexPath)

cell.textLabel?.text = items[indexPath.row]

return cell

}
```

6. Registering Cell Types

If you designed custom cells in Interface Builder, make sure to register them with the table view in viewDidLoad():

```
override func viewDidLoad() {

super.viewDidLoad()

tableView.register(UINib(nibName: "CustomCell", bundle: nil), forCellReuseIdentifier: "MyCellIdentifier")

}
```

7. Connecting Data Source and Delegate

In viewDidLoad(), set the table view's data source and delegate to the view controller:

```
override func viewDidLoad() {

super.viewDidLoad()

tableView.dataSource = self

tableView.delegate = self
```

}

8. Running the App

Build and run your app. You should see the table view populated with the data you provided in the items array.

This is a basic setup for creating a table view in iOS. You can further customize the appearance, handle user interactions, and add features like reordering and deleting rows to make your table view more interactive and user-friendly.

Section 9.2: Populating Data in Table Views

Once you've created a table view in your iOS app, the next step is populating it with data. This section covers various techniques for loading and displaying data in table views efficiently.

1. UITableViewDataSource Methods

In iOS, the UITableViewDataSource protocol defines methods that allow you to specify the content for each cell in your table view. The essential data source methods include:

- tableView(_:numberOfRowsInSection:): Returns the number of rows (cells) in a given section of the table view.
- tableView(_:cellForRowAt:): Provides the cell to display for a particular row.

Here's an example of how you can use these methods to populate a table view:

```
func tableView(_ tableView: UITableView, numberOfRowsInSection section: Int) -> Int {
```

return data.count *// Return the number of items in your data source*

}

func tableView(_ tableView: UITableView, cellForRowAt indexPath: IndexPath) -> UITableViewCell {

let cell = tableView.dequeueReusableCell(withIdentifier: "MyCellIdentifier", **for**: indexPath)

let item = data[indexPath.row] *// Get the data for the current row*

cell.textLabel?.text = item.title *// Set the cell's text label*

cell.detailTextLabel?.text = item.subtitle *// Set the cell's detail text label*

return cell

}

2. Data Source Updates

If your data source is dynamic and can change over time, you need to update the table view accordingly. Use methods like tableView.reloadData() to refresh the entire table view or tableView.insertRows(at:with:) and tableView.deleteRows(at:with:) to add or remove rows.

3. Sections and Grouping

You can organize your table view into sections to group related data. Implement the numberOfSections(in:) and tableView(_:titleForHeaderInSection:) methods to define the number of sections and their headers. This is useful for displaying data like contacts grouped by the first letter of their names.

```
func numberOfSections(in tableView: UITableView) -> Int {

return sectionTitles.count // Return the number of sections

}

func tableView(_ tableView: UITableView, titleForHeaderInSection section: Int) -> String? {

return sectionTitles[section] // Return the title for each section

}
```

4. Custom Cells

To display more complex data, you can create custom table view cells. Design these cells in Interface Builder or create them programmatically. Register custom cell classes or nibs using tableView.register(_:forCellReuseIdentifier:) in your view controller's viewDidLoad().

5. Asynchronous Data Loading

When fetching data from a remote server or performing time-consuming operations, it's essential to load data asynchronously to avoid blocking the main thread and keeping the user interface responsive. Libraries like URLSession can help you download data asynchronously and update the table view once the data is available.

6. Lazy Loading

If your data source contains a large number of items, consider implementing lazy loading. Only load and display a portion of the data initially, and load more as the user scrolls. This technique improves performance and reduces memory usage.

7. Pull-to-Refresh

For content that can change frequently, such as news feeds or social media timelines, you can add a pull-to-refresh control to your table view. This allows users to trigger a refresh manually by pulling down the table view.

8. Filtering and Search

Implementing filtering and search functionality in your table view can enhance the user experience. You can add a search bar to let users search for specific items within the table view, updating the displayed data based on search results.

In summary, populating data in table views is a fundamental aspect of iOS app development. By conforming to the UITableViewDataSource protocol, you can control the content and appearance of your table view cells. Additionally, consider advanced techniques like sections, custom cells, asynchronous data loading, lazy loading, pull-to-refresh, and filtering to create a smooth and user-friendly experience when working with table views in your iOS app.

Section 9.3: Customizing Table View Cells

Customizing table view cells allows you to create unique and visually appealing layouts for your app's content. This section explores various techniques for customizing table view cells in iOS development.

1. Using Interface Builder

Interface Builder provides a visual way to design custom table view cells. Follow these steps:

1. Create a new UITableViewCell subclass.
2. Design the cell's layout using Interface Builder, adding labels, images, buttons, or any other UI elements.
3. Set up outlets for UI elements in your custom cell class.
4. In your table view's data source method tableView(_:cellForRowAt:), dequeue and configure the custom cell.

Here's a simple example:

```
func tableView(_ tableView: UITableView, cellForRowAt indexPath: IndexPath) -> UITableViewCell {

let cell = tableView.dequeueReusableCell(withIdentifier: "CustomCellIdentifier", for: indexPath) as! CustomTableViewCell

let item = data[indexPath.row] // Get data for the current row

cell.titleLabel.text = item.title

cell.subtitleLabel.text = item.subtitle

return cell

}
```

2. Creating Custom Cells Programmatically

If you prefer to create custom cells programmatically, follow these steps:

1. Create a new UITableViewCell subclass.
2. Override the init(style:reuseIdentifier:) initializer to set up your cell's UI elements.
3. Configure the cell in the tableView(_:cellForRowAt:) data source method.

Here's an example:

```
class CustomTableViewCell: UITableViewCell {

let titleLabel = UILabel()

let subtitleLabel = UILabel()

override init(style: UITableViewCell.CellStyle, reuseIdentifier: String?) {

super.init(style: style, reuseIdentifier: reuseIdentifier)

// Customize UI elements and add them to the cell's contentView

}

required init?(coder aDecoder: NSCoder) {

fatalError("init(coder:) has not been implemented")

}

}
```

Then, in your data source method:

```
func tableView(_ tableView: UITableView, cellForRowAt indexPath: IndexPath) -> UITableViewCell {

let cell = tableView.dequeueReusableCell(withIdentifier: "CustomCellIdentifier", for: indexPath) as! CustomTableViewCell

let item = data[indexPath.row] // Get data for the current row

cell.titleLabel.text = item.title

cell.subtitleLabel.text = item.subtitle
```

return cell

}

3. Handling Cell Selection

You can customize the behavior when a cell is selected by implementing the tableView(_:didSelectRowAt:) delegate method. For example, you can navigate to another view controller, show additional details, or perform any desired action.

4. Dynamic Cell Heights

If your custom cells have varying heights, override the tableView(_:heightForRowAt:) data source method to return the appropriate height for each cell. This is common when displaying cells with variable content, such as text of different lengths or images with different aspect ratios.

5. Reusable Cell Identifiers

When using custom cells, make sure to register the cell class or nib with the table view using register(:forCellReuseIdentifier:) in your view controller's viewDidLoad() method. This ensures that the table view can dequeue cells correctly.

6. Separators and Backgrounds

You can customize the appearance of cell separators and backgrounds by setting properties like separatorStyle, separatorColor, and backgroundColor on the table view and individual cells.

Customizing table view cells allows you to create visually appealing and tailored user interfaces for your iOS app. Whether you use

Interface Builder or create custom cells programmatically, understanding these techniques will help you design compelling user experiences and present your app's content in a unique way.

Section 9.4: Implementing Collection Views

Collection views are versatile UI components in iOS that allow you to display content in a grid or custom layout. In this section, we'll explore how to implement collection views in your iOS app.

1. Collection View Basics

A collection view is an instance of UICollectionView and operates similarly to a table view. It consists of sections and items (cells) arranged in a grid-like manner. To get started, follow these steps:

- Create a new UICollectionView in your view controller's storyboard or create it programmatically.

2. Collection View Data Source

To populate a collection view, implement the UICollectionViewDataSource protocol. Key methods to implement include:

- numberOfSections(in collectionView: UICollectionView) -> Int: Return the number of sections in your collection view.
- collectionView(_:numberOfItemsInSection:) -> Int: Return the number of items (cells) in each section.

- collectionView(_:cellForItemAt:) -> UICollectionViewCell: Dequeue and configure the cell for a given index path.

Here's a simple example:

```
func collectionView(_ collectionView: UICollectionView, numberOfItemsInSection section: Int) -> Int {

return data.count // Replace with the actual number of items

}

func collectionView(_ collectionView: UICollectionView, cellForItemAt indexPath: IndexPath) -> UICollectionViewCell {

let cell = collectionView.dequeueReusableCell(withReuseIdentifier: "CustomCellIdentifier", for: indexPath) as! CustomCollectionViewCell

let item = data[indexPath.item] // Get data for the current item

cell.titleLabel.text = item.title

// Configure other cell properties here

return cell

}
```

3. Collection View Layout

You can choose from different layout classes (e.g., UICollectionViewFlowLayout, UICollectionViewCompositionalLayout) to define the appearance and arrangement of items within the collection view. Customize the layout to achieve the desired grid or custom arrangement.

4. Cell Customization

Similar to table view cells, you can create custom collection view cells by subclassing UICollectionViewCell. Customize the cell's UI and appearance to fit your app's design.

5. Handling Selection

Implement the collectionView(_:didSelectItemAt:) delegate method to respond to user interactions with collection view items. You can perform actions such as navigating to another view controller or displaying additional details.

6. Dynamic Cell Sizing

For variable-sized cells, implement the collectionView(_:layout:sizeForItemAt:) delegate method to return the size of each cell based on its content. This is useful when displaying items with different dimensions.

7. Section Headers and Footers

You can add headers and footers to sections in your collection view by implementing the appropriate data source methods (collectionView(_:viewForSupplementaryElementOfKind:at:)). This is handy for providing section titles or additional information.

8. Reusable Identifiers

Ensure that you register your custom cell class or nib with the collection view using register(_:forCellWithReuseIdentifier:). This allows the collection view to dequeue cells efficiently.

9. Reloading Data

When your data changes, call reloadData() on the collection view to refresh its content. You can also use more specific methods like insertItems(at:) or deleteItems(at:) to update the collection view incrementally.

10. UICollectionViewDelegateFlowLayout

The UICollectionViewDelegateFlowLayout protocol provides methods for fine-tuning layout behavior, such as setting minimum spacing between cells, defining section insets, and more.

Collection views are powerful tools for creating dynamic and flexible layouts in your iOS app. By understanding the basics of collection view data sources, layout customization, and cell management, you can efficiently display content in grid-like arrangements or implement custom layouts tailored to your app's requirements.

Section 9.5: Creating Dynamic Data Displays

Dynamic data displays are essential in many iOS apps, allowing users to interact with and manipulate data in real-time. In this section, we'll explore how to create dynamic data displays that update dynamically as data changes.

1. Using UITableView for Dynamic Lists

UITableView is a powerful tool for creating dynamic lists of data. To create a dynamic data display:

- Create a UITableView in your view controller.
- Implement the UITableViewDataSource protocol to provide data to the table view.

- Use the reloadData() method to refresh the table view when data changes.

Here's a basic example:

```
class DynamicListViewController: UIViewController, UITableViewDataSource {

@IBOutlet weak var tableView: UITableView!

var data = ["Item 1", "Item 2", "Item 3"]

override func viewDidLoad() {

super.viewDidLoad()

tableView.dataSource = self

}

func tableView(_ tableView: UITableView, numberOfRowsInSection section: Int) -> Int {

return data.count

}

func tableView(_ tableView: UITableView, cellForRowAt indexPath: IndexPath) -> UITableViewCell {

let cell = tableView.dequeueReusableCell(withIdentifier: "CellIdentifier", for: indexPath)

cell.textLabel?.text = data[indexPath.row]

return cell

}
```

```
// Implement methods for data manipulation, e.g., deleting rows, adding data.

}
```

2. Real-time Updates with UITableView

To update a UITableView in real-time when data changes, follow these steps:

- Modify the data source (e.g., add, remove, or update items).
- Call tableView.reloadData() on the main thread to refresh the table view.

For example, if you want to add a new item to the list:

```
func addItem(_ newItem: String) {

data.append(newItem)

DispatchQueue.main.async {

self.tableView.reloadData()

}

}
```

3. Using UICollectionView for Grid-Based Displays

For grid-based dynamic displays, use UICollectionView. The process is similar to UITableView:

- Create a UICollectionView in your view controller.

- Implement the UICollectionViewDataSource protocol.
- Call collectionView.reloadData() to update the collection view when data changes.

4. Real-time Updates with UICollectionView

To achieve real-time updates in a UICollectionView, update the data source and call collectionView.reloadData() on the main thread, just like with UITableView.

5. Using Observers for Data Changes

In more complex scenarios, consider using observers or reactive programming frameworks like Combine or RxSwift to automatically update your dynamic data displays when data changes. These tools provide elegant ways to handle data updates and UI synchronization.

6. Animations for Data Changes

To create smoother user experiences, apply animations when data changes. For instance, you can use insertItems(at:) and deleteItems(at:) methods for UICollectionView or row animation methods for UITableView to animate changes gracefully.

7. Managing Large Data Sets

If dealing with large data sets, consider pagination or lazy loading to efficiently load and display data as needed. This can improve app performance and user experience.

Dynamic data displays are fundamental in modern app development, providing users with real-time interactions and updates. By leveraging UITableView and UICollectionView, understanding how to update them in real-time, and exploring advanced techniques like animations and observables, you can create dynamic and engaging user interfaces that respond to changing data.

Chapter 10: Working with Navigation and Segues

Section 10.1: Navigation Controllers and Bar

In iOS app development, navigation is a fundamental concept. It enables users to move between different views or screens within your app. One common way to implement navigation is by using navigation controllers and navigation bars.

Understanding Navigation Controllers

A UINavigationController is a container view controller that manages a hierarchical stack of view controllers. It provides navigation functionalities like pushing and popping view controllers onto and from the stack.

Here's how to set up a basic navigation controller:

1. **Storyboard Setup:** In your storyboard, embed your initial view controller in a navigation controller. You can do this by selecting the view controller, then navigating to "Editor" -> "Embed In" -> "Navigation Controller."
2. **Programmatic Setup:** In code, you can create a navigation controller and set its root view controller.

```
// Creating a navigation controller and setting its root view controller

let rootViewController = UIViewController()

let navigationController = UINavigationController(rootViewController: rootViewController)
```

The Navigation Bar

The navigation bar is a UI component provided by the navigation controller. It typically appears at the top of the screen and contains elements like the title of the current view, navigation buttons, and the back button.

Here's how to customize the navigation bar:

- **Title:** You can set the title of a view controller that's part of the navigation stack using title property.

```
navigationItem.title = "My Screen Title"
```

- **Navigation Buttons:** You can add buttons to the navigation bar, like "Back," "Save," or "Done," by creating instances of UIBarButtonItem and assigning them to the navigationItem.rightBarButtonItem or navigationItem.leftBarButtonItem property.

```
let saveButton = UIBarButtonItem(title: "Save", style: .plain, target: self, action: #selector(saveTapped))

navigationItem.rightBarButtonItem = saveButton
```

- **Back Button:** By default, a back button is automatically added to the navigation bar when you push a view controller onto the stack. You can customize the back button's title using navigationItem.backBarButtonItem.

```
navigationItem.backBarButtonItem = UIBarButtonItem(title: "Back", style: .plain, target: nil, action: nil)
```

Navigation Stack

The navigation stack represents the hierarchy of view controllers managed by the navigation controller. You can push a new view controller onto the stack to navigate forward and pop the top view controller to navigate back.

```
// Pushing a new view controller onto the stack

let newViewController = UIViewController()

navigationController?.pushViewController(newViewController, animated: true)

// Popping the top view controller

navigationController?.popViewController(animated: true)
```

Navigation Segues

In a storyboard-based app, you can create segues to define transitions between view controllers. Segues are triggered by user actions, like tapping a button, and are a visual representation of navigation flows.

To create a segue:

1. Control-drag from a UI element (e.g., a button) to the destination view controller.
2. Choose the segue type (e.g., "Show," "Push," "Modal") and provide an identifier if needed.
3. Implement the prepare(for:sender:) method in the source view controller to pass data to the destination view controller before the segue.

```
override func prepare(for segue: UIStoryboardSegue, sender: Any?) {
```

```
if segue.identifier == "MySegueIdentifier" {
if let destinationVC = segue.destination as? MyDestinationViewController {
destinationVC.data = someData
}
}
}
```

Understanding navigation controllers and navigation bars is crucial for building iOS apps with effective user interfaces and navigation flows. Whether you're creating your navigation flow programmatically or using storyboards and segues, mastering these concepts will help you design intuitive and user-friendly apps.

Section 10.2: Creating Segues and Transitions

In iOS app development, segues are a way to define and manage transitions between view controllers. They are especially useful when you want to move from one screen to another, such as going from a list of items to a detailed view of a selected item. In this section, we'll explore how to create segues and manage transitions between view controllers.

Creating Segues in Storyboards

Storyboard-based development makes it easy to create and visualize segues. Here's how to create a segue:

1. **Control-Drag:** In your storyboard, control-drag from a

UI element, such as a button, to the destination view controller. This action will bring up a context menu.

2. **Choose Segue Type:** From the context menu, choose the type of segue you want to create. The available segue types include "Show," "Show Detail," "Present Modally," "Popover Presentation," and more.
3. **Identifier (Optional):** You can provide an identifier for the segue if you need to perform some action or customization in code before the transition. To set an identifier, select the segue in the storyboard and enter a unique identifier in the Attributes Inspector.
4. **Implement prepare(for:sender:) Method:** To pass data from the source view controller to the destination view controller before the segue, implement the prepare(for:sender:) method in the source view controller.

```
override func prepare(for segue: UIStoryboardSegue, sender: Any?) {

if segue.identifier == "MySegueIdentifier" {

if let destinationVC = segue.destination as? MyDestinationViewController {

destinationVC.data = someData

}

}

}
```

Programmatic Segue Creation

While storyboards are a powerful way to create segues visually, you can also create segues programmatically when needed. This approach is useful when you want to trigger a segue based on some condition or user interaction.

To programmatically perform a segue, you can use the performSegue(withIdentifier:sender:) method:

```
performSegue(withIdentifier: "MySegueIdentifier", sender: self)
```

Unwind Segues

Unwind segues allow you to transition back to a previous view controller in your navigation stack. They are typically used in scenarios where you want to dismiss a presented view controller and return to a specific view controller in the hierarchy.

To create an unwind segue:

1. In the destination view controller (the one you want to unwind to), create an @IBAction method that takes a UIStoryboardSegue as a parameter. This method will be the target for the unwind segue.

```
@IBAction func unwindToPreviousViewController(segue: UIStoryboardSegue) {

// Perform any necessary actions when unwinding

}
```

1. In the source view controller, control-drag from a UI element to the “Exit” icon of the view controller scene in the storyboard. You’ll see a list of available unwind segues,

including the one you created. Select the unwind segue you want to use.

Custom Segue Transitions

In some cases, you may want to create custom transitions between view controllers. This can involve animations, special effects, or unique navigation flows. To achieve custom transitions, you can subclass UIStoryboardSegue and override its perform() method to define your custom behavior.

```
class CustomSegue: UIStoryboardSegue {

override func perform() {

// Implement your custom transition logic here

}

}
```

Creating and managing segues is a fundamental skill in iOS development, enabling you to control the flow of your app and create smooth transitions between screens. Whether you're using storyboards for visual segue creation or programmatically triggering segues, understanding this concept is crucial for building intuitive and engaging iOS apps.

Section 10.3: Passing Data Between View Controllers

Passing data between view controllers is a common task in iOS app development. You often need to send information from one view controller to another to display or process it. In this section, we'll explore various techniques for passing data between view controllers.

1. Segue-Based Data Transfer

One of the most common methods to pass data between view controllers is through segues. Here's a step-by-step guide on how to do this:

1. Create a segue between the source and destination view controllers in the storyboard.
2. Give the segue an identifier in the Attributes Inspector. This identifier will be used to identify the segue in code.
3. Implement the prepare(for:sender:) method in the source view controller. This method is called just before the segue occurs and allows you to configure the destination view controller.

```
override func prepare(for segue: UIStoryboardSegue, sender: Any?) {

if segue.identifier == "MySegueIdentifier" {

if let destinationVC = segue.destination as? MyDestinationViewController {

destinationVC.data = someData

}

}

}
```

1. In the destination view controller, create a property to receive the data, like var data: DataType?. You can then use this property to access the passed data.

2. Delegation

Delegation is another powerful way to pass data between view controllers. It involves defining a protocol and delegate relationship between the source and destination view controllers. Here's how it works:

1. Define a protocol in the source view controller that includes methods for passing data.

```
protocol DataPassingDelegate: AnyObject {

func passData(data: DataType)

}
```

1. Create a delegate property in the source view controller.

```
weak var delegate: DataPassingDelegate?
```

1. In the destination view controller, conform to the protocol.

```
class DestinationViewController: UIViewController, DataPassingDelegate {

// ...

}
```

1. Implement the protocol methods in the destination view controller to receive and process the data.

```
func passData(data: DataType) {

// Handle the passed data
```

```
}
```

1. Before navigating to the destination view controller, set the delegate property of the destination view controller to self in the source view controller.

```
destinationVC.delegate = self
```

1. Finally, call the delegate method in the source view controller to pass the data.

3. Singleton

A singleton is a design pattern that ensures a class has only one instance and provides a global point of access to it. You can use a singleton to store and retrieve data that needs to be shared between multiple view controllers.

1. Create a singleton class that holds the data you want to share.

```
class DataSingleton {

static let shared = DataSingleton()

var sharedData: DataType?

}
```

1. In the source view controller, set the data in the singleton.

```
DataSingleton.shared.sharedData = someData
```

1. In the destination view controller, retrieve the data from the singleton.

```
let data = DataSingleton.shared.sharedData
```

4. UserDefaults

UserDefaults is a simple way to persist small amounts of data between app launches. It can be used to store and retrieve data between view controllers.

1. Save the data to UserDefaults in the source view controller.

```
UserDefaults.standard.set(someData, forKey: "KeyForData")
```

1. Retrieve the data from UserDefaults in the destination view controller.

```
if let data = UserDefaults.standard.object(forKey: "KeyForData") as? DataType {

// Use the retrieved data

}
```

Each of these methods has its use cases, and the choice of which one to use depends on the specific requirements of your app. Select the approach that best fits your data passing needs for a particular scenario.

Section 10.4: Implementing Navigation Patterns

Navigation within an iOS app is a critical aspect of providing a seamless user experience. In this section, we'll explore various navigation patterns and techniques commonly used in iOS app development.

1. Linear Navigation

Linear navigation is a simple and straightforward navigation pattern. In this pattern, the user progresses through a series of view controllers in a linear sequence, typically following a specific flow or order. It's often used in onboarding processes, tutorials, or form-based workflows.

To implement linear navigation, you can use techniques like push segues or modal presentation, where each new view controller is presented over the previous one. Use the UINavigationController for push segues to provide a built-in navigation bar for moving forward and backward in the sequence.

2. Tab Bar Navigation

Tab bar navigation is a widely used pattern for organizing and switching between different sections or functionalities within an app. It's represented by a tab bar at the bottom of the screen, with each tab corresponding to a specific view controller or feature.

To implement tab bar navigation, you need to create a UITabBarController. Each tab is associated with a view controller, and users can switch between them by tapping on the corresponding tab. Tab bar navigation is suitable for apps with distinct sections or modes, such as social media apps (e.g., Home, Profile, Notifications) or productivity apps (e.g., Tasks, Calendar, Notes).

3. Master-Detail Navigation

The master-detail navigation pattern is commonly used for displaying lists of items and their details. It's prevalent in apps like email clients, news readers, or contact managers.

In this pattern, there are two main view controllers:

- **Master View Controller**: This view controller displays a list of items. When an item is selected, it shows its details in the detail view controller.

- **Detail View Controller**: This view controller displays the details of the selected item. It's updated based on the item selected in the master view.

To implement master-detail navigation, you can use a UISplitViewController for iPads or implement a custom master-detail interface for iPhones. This pattern allows users to easily browse through lists and view detailed information.

4. Navigation Drawer (Side Menu)

The navigation drawer, also known as the side menu, is a navigation pattern often used to provide access to app features or sections through a hidden panel that can be swiped or tapped to reveal. It's commonly seen in apps like Gmail or Facebook.

To implement a navigation drawer, you can use third-party libraries or create a custom solution. It typically involves a container view controller that manages the side menu and the main content area. Users can access different sections of the app by opening the side menu and selecting an option.

5. Modal Presentation

Modal presentation is a navigation pattern used for displaying temporary or context-specific view controllers on top of the current view controller. Modals are often used for tasks like user authentication, settings, or composing new content.

To present a view controller modally, you can use the present(_:animated:completion:) method. Modal view controllers can be dismissed by the user or programmatically.

6. Custom Transitions

Custom transitions allow you to create unique and visually appealing navigation experiences. You can implement custom transitions to provide animations and interactions that go beyond the standard push or modal presentation.

To create custom transitions, you need to conform to the UIViewControllerAnimatedTransitioning protocol and provide custom animations and interaction controllers. Custom transitions are often used in apps with rich visual experiences or games.

In your iOS app, the choice of navigation pattern depends on your app's structure, content, and user experience goals. You may also use a combination of these patterns to create a user-friendly and efficient navigation flow. Consider the specific needs of your app and its users when designing your navigation system.

Section 10.5: Building Navigation-Based Apps

Navigation-based apps play a significant role in providing a structured and intuitive user experience. In this section, we'll delve into building navigation-based apps in iOS using various components and techniques.

1. UINavigationController

The UINavigationController class is at the heart of building navigation-based apps in iOS. It provides a navigation stack that manages a hierarchy of view controllers. Each view controller represents a screen or a page in the app. The navigation controller's stack allows users to navigate forward and backward through the app's content.

Here's how to set up a basic UINavigationController:

```
// Create your view controllers

let viewController1 = UIViewController()

let viewController2 = UIViewController()

// Initialize the navigation controller with a root view controller

let navigationController = UINavigationController(rootViewController: viewController1)

// Push a new view controller onto the navigation stack

navigationController.pushViewController(viewController2, animated: true)
```

2. Navigation Bar

The navigation bar is a crucial component of navigation-based apps. It typically appears at the top of the screen and contains navigation items such as the back button, title, and optional buttons. You can customize the navigation bar's appearance and content to match your app's design.

```
// Set the title for the current view controller

viewController1.title = "Home"

// Add a custom button to the navigation bar

let settingsButton = UIBarButtonItem(image: UIImage(named: "settings"), style: .plain, target: self, action: #selector(showSettings))

viewController1.navigationItem.rightBarButtonItem = settingsButton
```

3. Pushing and Popping View Controllers

Navigation controllers manage a stack of view controllers. You can push new view controllers onto the stack to navigate forward and pop view controllers to go back.

```
// Push a new view controller onto the stack

let newViewController = UIViewController()

navigationController.pushViewController(newViewController, animated: true)

// Pop the current view controller to go back

navigationController.popViewController(animated: true)
```

4. Tab Bar Controller

In some cases, navigation-based apps are combined with tab bar controllers. A UITabBarController allows users to switch between different sections or features of the app using tabs at the bottom of the screen. Each tab can contain its navigation controller and stack of view controllers.

```
// Create view controllers for each tab

let homeViewController = UINavigationController(rootViewController: HomeViewController())

let settingsViewController = UINavigationController(rootViewController: SettingsViewController())

// Create a tab bar controller

let tabBarController = UITabBarController()

tabBarController.viewControllers = [homeViewController, settingsViewController]
```

5. Navigation Patterns

Navigation-based apps often follow specific navigation patterns, such as linear navigation, master-detail, or tab bar navigation, as discussed in previous chapters. Choosing the right navigation pattern depends on your app's structure and user experience requirements.

6. Custom Transitions

For advanced navigation experiences, you can implement custom view controller transitions. Custom transitions allow you to create unique animations and interactions when pushing or popping view controllers.

To create custom transitions, you need to implement the UIViewControllerAnimatedTransitioning protocol and specify the animations for presenting and dismissing view controllers.

```
class CustomTransition: NSObject, UIViewControllerAnimatedTransitioning {

// Implement custom transition animations

}
```

Building navigation-based apps in iOS requires careful consideration of the app's structure and user flow. By utilizing UINavigationController, customizing the navigation bar, and choosing the appropriate navigation patterns, you can create a seamless and user-friendly navigation experience for your iOS app.

Chapter 11: Building Interactive Forms

Section 11.1: Designing User Input Forms

In the world of mobile app development, creating user input forms is a common task. Forms allow users to provide information, make choices, and interact with your app. Whether you're building a registration page, a survey, or a settings screen, designing effective and user-friendly forms is essential.

The Importance of Form Design

Designing user input forms might seem straightforward, but it requires careful consideration. A well-designed form can enhance user experience, improve data accuracy, and even boost conversion rates. On the other hand, a poorly designed form can frustrate users, leading to abandonment and errors.

Here are some key considerations for designing user input forms:

1. **Clarity and Simplicity**: Forms should be easy to understand. Use clear labels and concise instructions to guide users.
2. **Relevance**: Only ask for information that is necessary. Avoid overwhelming users with too many fields.
3. **Logical Flow**: Organize fields logically, following a natural order or sequence of tasks.
4. **Error Handling**: Provide helpful error messages and validation to prevent user mistakes.
5. **Mobile-Friendly**: Ensure that your forms are responsive and work well on mobile devices.
6. **Accessibility**: Design forms that are accessible to users with disabilities, including proper labeling and ARIA

attributes.

Design Elements for Forms

To create effective user input forms, you'll need to use various design elements and components:

1. Text Fields

Text fields are used for inputting text-based information. They can be single-line or multi-line and are commonly used for things like names, email addresses, and comments.

```
// Example of a single-line text field in Swift using SwiftUI

TextField("Enter your name", text: $name)

.textFieldStyle(RoundedBorderTextFieldStyle())
```

2. Checkboxes and Radio Buttons

Checkboxes allow users to select multiple options, while radio buttons allow single selections. They are often used for multiple-choice questions or settings.

```
// Example of checkboxes in SwiftUI

Toggle("Subscribe to newsletter", isOn: $subscribe)

// Example of radio buttons in SwiftUI

Picker("Gender", selection: $selectedGender) {

ForEach(Gender.allCases, id: \.self) { gender in

Text(gender.rawValue).tag(gender)
```

```
}
}
.pickerStyle(RadioGroupPickerStyle())
```

3. Dropdowns and Pickers

Dropdowns and pickers provide a list of options for users to choose from. They are space-efficient and work well for long lists of choices.

```
// Example of a picker in SwiftUI
Picker("Country", selection: $selectedCountry) {
ForEach(countries, id: \.self) { country in
Text(country)
}
}
.pickerStyle(DefaultPickerStyle())
```

4. Buttons

Buttons are used for actions like form submission or resetting. They should be clearly labeled and easily distinguishable from other elements.

```
// Example of a submit button in SwiftUI
Button(action: submitForm) {
Text("Submit")
```

```
.padding()
.background(Color.blue)
.foregroundColor(.white)
.cornerRadius(8)
}
```

5. Labels and Instructions

Labels provide context for form fields, while instructions guide users on how to fill out the form correctly.

```
// Example of labels and instructions in SwiftUI
VStack(alignment: .leading) {
Text("Email Address")
.font(.headline)
TextField("Enter your email", text: $email)
.textFieldStyle(RoundedBorderTextFieldStyle())
Text("We'll send important updates to this email.")
.font(.subheadline)
.foregroundColor(.gray)
}
```

User-Centered Design

Remember that the goal of your form is to make it as easy as possible for users to provide the information you need. Conduct user testing and gather feedback to refine your form's design and usability. By putting users at the center of your design process, you can create forms that are intuitive and effective.

Designing user input forms is a critical skill for iOS developers, and mastering this skill will lead to better user engagement and satisfaction with your apps.

Section 11.2: Validating User Input

User input validation is a crucial aspect of form design in iOS app development. Validating user input ensures that the data submitted through your forms is accurate, consistent, and secure. In this section, we'll explore various validation techniques and best practices.

Why User Input Validation Matters

User input can be unpredictable, and users may unintentionally or intentionally submit incorrect or malicious data. Validating user input helps in several ways:

1. **Data Accuracy**: Validation ensures that the data entered matches the expected format and criteria. For example, it verifies that an email address contains "@" and a valid domain.
2. **Security**: Proper validation helps protect your app from security vulnerabilities such as SQL injection or cross-site scripting (XSS) attacks.
3. **User Experience**: Detecting errors early and providing

clear feedback improves the user experience by preventing frustration and confusion.

Common Validation Techniques

1. Required Fields

Ensure that mandatory fields are filled out. You can mark them with asterisks or other indicators and display an error message if a user tries to submit without completing them.

```
if name.isEmpty || email.isEmpty {
// Show an error message
}
```

2. Format Validation

Check that data follows the expected format. For example, use regular expressions to validate email addresses or phone numbers.

```
let emailRegex = "[A-Z0-9a-z._%+-]+@[A-Za-z0-9.-]+\\.[A-Za-z]{2,}"
if !NSPredicate(format: "SELF MATCHES %@", emailRegex).evaluate(with: email) {
// Show an error for an invalid email format
}
```

3. Length Validation

Limit the length of input for specific fields, such as passwords or usernames. Display character count and enforce maximum length.

```
if password.count < 6 {
// Show an error for a too-short password
}
```

4. Range Validation

Ensure that numeric input falls within acceptable ranges. For instance, validate that a user's age is between 18 and 99.

```
if age < 18 || age > 99 {
// Show an error for an invalid age
}
```

5. Confirmation Fields

For sensitive data like passwords or email addresses, include a confirmation field and compare it with the original input.

```
if password != confirmPassword {
// Show an error for password mismatch
}
```

Providing Clear Feedback

When validation fails, it's essential to provide users with clear and specific feedback. This feedback should:

- Highlight the field with the error.
- Explain the issue in plain language.
- Suggest how to correct the error.

```
// Example of displaying an error message in SwiftUI
if isInvalid {
Text("Please enter a valid email address.")
.foregroundColor(.red)
}
```

Server-Side Validation

While client-side validation is essential for a responsive user experience, server-side validation is equally critical for security. Client-side validation can be bypassed, so always validate user input on the server to ensure the integrity of your data.

Testing and Iteration

User input validation should be thoroughly tested, and the validation logic should be part of your unit and integration tests. Continuously gather user feedback and iterate on your validation process to improve the user experience and security of your app.

In summary, user input validation is a vital component of form design in iOS app development. It ensures data accuracy, enhances security, and improves the user experience. By implementing various validation techniques and providing clear feedback, you can create forms that collect reliable and secure data from your users.

Section 11.3: Handling Form Submission

Handling form submission is a critical aspect of iOS app development, particularly when building apps that require users to submit data or perform actions. In this section, we'll explore the key considerations and best practices for handling form submissions effectively.

Understanding the Form Submission Workflow

Before diving into the technical aspects, let's understand the typical workflow of handling form submissions in an iOS app:

1. **User Interaction**: A user interacts with the app's user interface, filling out various form fields and providing input.
2. **Validation**: As discussed in the previous sections, it's essential to validate user input to ensure that it meets the required criteria and is secure.
3. **Data Preparation**: Once input data passes validation, it should be prepared for submission. This may involve converting data types, encoding, or formatting.
4. **Submission**: The prepared data is sent to a server or backend system for processing. This could involve making HTTP requests to APIs or databases.
5. **Response Handling**: After submission, the app receives a response from the server. This response may indicate success, failure, or other relevant information.
6. **Feedback to User**: Based on the server's response, the app

should provide appropriate feedback to the user. This could include success messages, error messages, or redirection to different screens.

Implementing Form Submission

Here are the steps to implement form submission in your iOS app:

1. Define Submission Logic

Decide how and where you will handle form submissions. This might involve writing functions or methods to handle different types of submissions, such as user registration, data updates, or search queries.

```
func submitRegistrationForm(username: String, email: String, password: String) {
// Implement submission logic here
}
```

2. Capture User Input

In your app's user interface, capture user input using appropriate UI elements like text fields, buttons, and pickers. Use delegates or actions to trigger submission logic when the user interacts with the form.

```
@IBAction func submitButtonTapped(_ sender: UIButton) {
let username = usernameTextField.text ?? ""
let email = emailTextField.text ?? ""
```

let password = passwordTextField.text ?? ""

submitRegistrationForm(username: username, email: email, password: password)

}

3. Prepare and Send Data

Before sending data to the server, ensure it's properly prepared. This may involve creating JSON objects, encoding parameters, or attaching authentication tokens.

func prepareAndSendData(username: String, email: String, password: String) {

let parameters: [String: Any] = [

"username": username,

"email": email,

"password": password

]

// Encode parameters and make an HTTP request

// (e.g., using URLSession or Alamofire)

}

4. Handle Server Response

Once the server processes the data, it sends a response. Handle the response appropriately, checking for success and displaying relevant messages to the user.

```
func handleServerResponse(response: ServerResponse) {

if response.isSuccess {

// Show a success message and potentially navigate to a new screen

} else {

// Show an error message to the user

}

}
```

5. Provide Feedback

User feedback is crucial. Inform the user about the outcome of the form submission. This can be done by updating UI elements with success or error messages.

```
func showFeedback(message: String, isError: Bool) {

feedbackLabel.text = message

feedbackLabel.textColor = isError ? .red : .green

}
```

Asynchronous Operations

Keep in mind that form submissions often involve asynchronous operations, such as making network requests. Ensure that your code handles asynchronous operations gracefully, using techniques like completion handlers or async/await if you're using Swift concurrency.

In summary, handling form submissions in iOS apps requires careful planning and implementation. By understanding the workflow, implementing submission logic, capturing user input, preparing and sending data, handling server responses, and providing clear feedback, you can create a robust and user-friendly form submission process in your app.

Section 11.4: Enhancing User Experience

Enhancing the user experience (UX) is a crucial aspect of building interactive forms in iOS applications. An excellent user experience not only ensures that your app is user-friendly but also helps in improving user engagement and satisfaction. In this section, we'll explore some strategies and best practices for enhancing the user experience when dealing with forms.

1. Real-Time Validation

Implement real-time validation of user input. As users fill out form fields, provide immediate feedback on whether their input is valid. For example, you can highlight input fields with red borders or display error messages next to fields with invalid data.

```
func validateUsername(_ username: String) -> Bool {

// Implement username validation logic
```

```
}

usernameTextField.addTarget(self, action: #selector(usernameChanged(_:)), for: .editingChanged)

@objc func usernameChanged(_ textField: UITextField) {

if let text = textField.text {

let isValid = validateUsername(text)

textField.layer.borderColor = isValid ? UIColor.green.cgColor : UIColor.red.cgColor

}

}
```

2. Keyboard Management

Manage the keyboard intelligently to prevent it from obstructing form fields. Use the UIScrollView or UITableView content insets to adjust the content view's position when the keyboard appears. This ensures that the active input field is visible.

```
NotificationCenter.default.addObserver(

self,

selector: #selector(keyboardWillShow(_:)),

name: UIResponder.keyboardWillShowNotification,

object: nil

)

@objc func keyboardWillShow(_ notification: Notification) {
```

```
if let userInfo = notification.userInfo,

let keyboardFrame = userInfo[UIResponder.keyboardFrameEndUserInfoKey] as? CGRect {

let contentInsets = UIEdgeInsets(top: 0, left: 0, bottom: keyboardFrame.height, right: 0)

scrollView.contentInset = contentInsets

scrollView.scrollIndicatorInsets = contentInsets

}

}
```

3. Input Accessory Views

Consider adding custom input accessory views to make data entry more convenient. These accessory views can include "Next" and "Previous" buttons to navigate between form fields, a "Done" button to dismiss the keyboard, or even additional controls specific to your app's needs.

```
let toolbar = UIToolbar()

let prevButton = UIBarButtonItem(title: "Previous", style: .plain, target: self, action: #selector(previousField))

let nextButton = UIBarButtonItem(title: "Next", style: .plain, target: self, action: #selector(nextField))

let doneButton = UIBarButtonItem(title: "Done", style: .done, target: self, action: #selector(dismissKeyboard))
```

```
toolbar.items = [prevButton, nextButton, UIBarButtonItem.flexibleSpace, doneButton]

textField.inputAccessoryView = toolbar
```

4. Autocapitalization and Autocorrection

Set appropriate autocapitalization and autocorrection properties for text fields. For example, you can disable autocapitalization for email addresses or enable autocorrection for text inputs. This ensures that user input aligns with their expectations.

```
textField.autocapitalizationType = .none

textField.autocorrectionType = .yes
```

5. Clear and Reset Buttons

Consider adding "Clear" and "Reset" buttons to form fields, allowing users to quickly clear the content or reset the entire form. These buttons can save users time and frustration when they want to start over or correct a mistake.

```
let clearButton = UIButton(type: .custom)

clearButton.setImage(UIImage(named: "clear_icon"), for: .normal)

clearButton.frame = CGRect(x: 0, y: 0, width: 20, height: 20)

clearButton.addTarget(self, action: #selector(clearField), for: .touchUpInside)

textField.rightView = clearButton

textField.rightViewMode = .whileEditing
```

6. Error Handling

Handle errors gracefully by providing clear and specific error messages when form submissions fail. Avoid generic error messages and guide users on how to correct their input. Additionally, highlight the fields with errors to draw the user's attention.

```
func handleSubmissionError(error: Error) {

errorLabel.text = "An error occurred: \(error.localizedDescription)"

errorLabel.isHidden = false

// Highlight fields with errors

}
```

Enhancing the user experience in your iOS app's forms is an ongoing process. Continuously gather user feedback and iterate on your design and functionality to ensure that users find your forms easy to use and error-resistant. By following these best practices, you can create a seamless and user-friendly form-filling experience in your app.

Section 11.5: Building Forms for Data Entry

Building forms for data entry is a common requirement in iOS app development. Forms are used to collect user information, preferences, and input, making them a fundamental part of many applications. In this section, we will explore the best practices for designing and implementing forms that provide a smooth and intuitive user experience.

1. Define Clear Objectives

Before creating a form, define the clear objectives of the data you want to collect. Know what information is essential and relevant to your app's functionality. Avoid overwhelming users with unnecessary fields. Keep the form concise and focused on its purpose.

2. Group Related Fields

Group related fields together to create logical sections within the form. For example, personal information such as name, email, and phone number can be grouped under a "Contact Information" section. Grouping makes it easier for users to navigate and understand the form's structure.

3. Use the Appropriate Input Controls

Choose the appropriate input controls for each type of data. iOS provides various input controls such as text fields, text views, date pickers, and segmented controls. Use these controls to match the type of data you are collecting. For example, use a date picker for date of birth input and a segmented control for yes/no questions.

```
let datePicker = UIDatePicker()

datePicker.datePickerMode = .date

datePicker.addTarget(self, action: #selector(datePickerValueChanged(_:)), for: .valueChanged)

func datePickerValueChanged(_ sender: UIDatePicker) {

let dateFormatter = DateFormatter()

dateFormatter.dateFormat = "dd/MM/yyyy"
```

```
dateTextField.text = dateFormatter.string(from: sender.date)

}
```

4. Provide Clear Labels and Instructions

Label each form field clearly so users understand what information is expected. Additionally, you can provide instructions or placeholders to guide users on how to fill out specific fields. Clear labeling reduces user confusion and errors.

```
let nameLabel = UILabel()

nameLabel.text = "Full Name"

let emailLabel = UILabel()

emailLabel.text = "Email Address"
```

5. Use Input Validation

Implement input validation to ensure that users provide valid data. For example, validate email addresses, check for required fields, and verify the format of input such as phone numbers or postal codes. Display clear error messages when validation fails.

```
func validateEmail(_ email: String) -> Bool {

// Implement email validation logic

}

@IBAction func submitButtonTapped(_ sender: UIButton) {

if let email = emailTextField.text, !validateEmail(email) {

showError(message: "Invalid email address")
```

```
return
}
// Process the form data
}
func showError(message: String) {
// Display error message to the user
}
```

6. Handle Form Submission

Implement a clear and user-friendly way to submit the form. This could involve a "Submit" button that triggers the submission process. Ensure that the submission process is smooth and provides feedback to the user, such as a confirmation message.

```
@IBAction func submitButtonTapped(_ sender: UIButton) {
// Validate and process form data
if isValidForm() {
showConfirmation()
} else {
showError(message: "Please fill out all required fields.")
}
}
```

7. Support Accessibility

Make your forms accessible to users with disabilities. Use proper accessibility labels, hints, and traits to ensure that screen readers can convey the form's structure and purpose to users who rely on assistive technologies.

textField.accessibilityLabel = "Email Address"

textField.accessibilityHint = "Enter your email address"

8. Test on Multiple Devices

Test your forms on various iOS devices and screen sizes to ensure they are responsive and work correctly. Pay attention to how the form layout adapts to different orientations and devices, such as iPhones and iPads.

Building effective forms for data entry is essential for a positive user experience in your iOS app. By following these best practices and considering the needs of your target users, you can create forms that are intuitive, error-resistant, and accessible, contributing to the overall success of your application.

Chapter 12: Animations and Visual Effects

In this chapter, we will dive into the exciting world of animations and visual effects in iOS app development. Animations play a crucial role in enhancing the user experience, making your app more engaging and intuitive. We will explore various techniques and tools available in iOS to create animations and add visual effects to your app's user interface.

Section 12.1: Basic Animations in iOS

Animations bring your app's user interface to life, making it more interactive and appealing. Basic animations involve changing the properties of views or layers over a period of time to create smooth transitions and effects. Here, we'll explore the fundamentals of basic animations in iOS.

UIView Animations

UIView provides a simple way to perform basic animations in iOS. You can animate properties such as position, size, alpha (transparency), and more. Here's an example of animating a view's alpha (opacity):

```
UIView.animate(withDuration: 0.5) {

// Change the alpha property to make the view fade in

self.myView.alpha = 1.0

}
```

In this example, the alpha property of myView is animated to 1.0 (fully opaque) over a duration of 0.5 seconds.

Property Animations

You can animate any animatable property of a view using UIView.animate. Some common properties include frame, center, transform, and backgroundColor. For example, animating a view's position:

```
UIView.animate(withDuration: 0.5) {
```

```
// Change the view's center property to move it

self.myView.center = CGPoint(x: 200, y: 200)

}
```

Options and Completion Handlers

UIView.animate provides options for customizing the animation's behavior, such as timing curves and autoreverse. You can also specify a completion handler that executes code when the animation finishes:

```
UIView.animate(withDuration: 0.5, delay: 0.0, options: .curveEaseInOut, animations: {

// Your animation code here

}, completion: { finished in

if finished {

// Animation completed successfully

}

})
```

View Transitions

You can use view transitions to animate the addition or removal of views in your interface. For example, to fade in a new view:

```
UIView.transition(with: containerView, duration: 0.5, options: .transitionCrossDissolve, animations: {
```

self.containerView.addSubview(newView)

}, completion: **nil**)

In this example, transitionCrossDissolve is used to smoothly fade in the new view.

Keyframe Animations

Keyframe animations allow you to create complex animations with multiple steps and keyframes. You can use UIView.animateKeyframes to define keyframe animations:

UIView.animateKeyframes(withDuration: 2.0, delay: 0, options: [], animations: {

UIView.addKeyframe(withRelativeStartTime: 0, relativeDuration: 0.5) {

// Animation step 1

}

UIView.addKeyframe(withRelativeStartTime: 0.5, relativeDuration: 0.5) {

// Animation step 2

}

}, completion: **nil**)

These are some of the basics of creating animations in iOS using UIView. Animations can greatly enhance the user experience by providing visual feedback and guiding users through your app's interface. In the following sections, we will explore more advanced animation techniques and visual effects to take your iOS app's user interface to the next level.

Section 12.2: Advanced Animation Techniques

In the previous section, we covered the basics of animations in iOS using UIView. In this section, we'll delve deeper into advanced animation techniques and explore more sophisticated ways to create engaging animations in your iOS apps.

1. Spring Animations

Spring animations provide a more natural and bouncy feel to your animations. You can use the UIView.animate method with the .spring option to create spring animations. Here's an example:

```
UIView.animate(withDuration: 1.0, delay: 0, usingSpringWithDamping: 0.7, initialSpringVelocity: 0.5, options: [], animations: {

// Animation code here

}, completion: nil)
```

In this example, usingSpringWithDamping controls how "springy" the animation feels, and initialSpringVelocity determines the initial velocity of the animation.

2. CAAnimation and Core Animation

Core Animation is a powerful framework for creating complex animations. You can use CAAnimation subclasses to animate properties of layers. Here's a simple example of animating a layer's position:

```
let animation = CABasicAnimation(keyPath: "position")

animation.fromValue = CGPoint(x: 100, y: 100)

animation.toValue = CGPoint(x: 200, y: 200)

animation.duration = 1.0

myLayer.add(animation, forKey: "positionAnimation")
```

In this code, we create a basic animation for the layer's position and add it to the layer.

3. Keyframe Animations with Core Animation

Keyframe animations in Core Animation allow you to create animations with multiple keyframes and custom timing. Here's an example of animating a layer's position along a path:

```
let animation = CAKeyframeAnimation(keyPath: "position")

animation.path = customPath.cgPath

animation.duration = 2.0

animation.rotationMode = .rotateAuto

myLayer.add(animation, forKey: "positionPathAnimation")
```

In this example, customPath defines the path along which the layer's position animates.

4. Implicit Animations

Core Animation also supports implicit animations. These are animations that occur automatically when you change a layer's property. For example, changing a layer's background color:

CATransaction.begin()

CATransaction.setAnimationDuration(1.0)

myLayer.backgroundColor = UIColor.blue.cgColor

CATransaction.commit()

In this code, we wrap the property change in a CATransaction to control the animation's duration.

5. UIViewPropertyAnimator

iOS 10 introduced UIViewPropertyAnimator, which provides fine-grained control over animations, including pausing, reversing, and scrubbing. Here's a basic example:

let animator = UIViewPropertyAnimator(duration: 2.0, curve: .easeInOut) {

// Animation code here

}

animator.startAnimation()

UIViewPropertyAnimator offers advanced features for interactive animations, making it suitable for creating complex and interactive user interface animations.

These advanced animation techniques give you the tools to create rich and interactive animations in your iOS apps. Experiment with these techniques to enhance your app's user experience and make it more visually engaging. In the next section, we'll explore how to implement visual effects to further enhance your app's interface.

Section 12.3: Implementing Visual Effects

Visual effects can significantly improve the user experience in your iOS app by adding depth, realism, and interactivity. In this section, we'll explore various techniques for implementing visual effects.

1. Blur Effect

Adding a blur effect to your app's user interface elements can create a sense of depth and focus. You can use the UIVisualEffectView class to apply blur effects. Here's an example of adding a blur effect to a view:

```
let blurEffect = UIBlurEffect(style: .light)

let blurView = UIVisualEffectView(effect: blurEffect)

blurView.frame = CGRect(x: 0, y: 0, width: 200, height: 200)

// Add the blur view as a subview to your content view

myContentView.addSubview(blurView)
```

You can adjust the blur style (.light, .dark, .extraLight, etc.) to match your app's design.

2. Shadow Effects

Shadows can provide a sense of elevation and depth to your UI elements. You can add shadows to views by modifying their layer properties:

```
myView.layer.shadowColor = UIColor.black.cgColor

myView.layer.shadowOpacity = 0.5

myView.layer.shadowOffset = CGSize(width: 2, height: 2)
```

myView.layer.shadowRadius = 4.0

In this example, we create a subtle shadow effect for myView.

3. Gradient Backgrounds

Gradient backgrounds can make your app's interface more visually appealing. You can use the CAGradientLayer class to add gradients to views. Here's a simple gradient background:

```
let gradientLayer = CAGradientLayer()

gradientLayer.frame = myView.bounds

gradientLayer.colors = [UIColor.red.cgColor, UIColor.blue.cgColor]

myView.layer.insertSublayer(gradientLayer, at: 0)
```

This code creates a gradient that transitions from red to blue.

4. Parallax Effects

Parallax effects involve moving UI elements at different speeds to create a sense of depth. You can implement parallax effects using the UIInterpolatingMotionEffect class. Here's how to add a parallax effect to a view:

```
let horizontalMotionEffect = UIInterpolatingMotionEffect(keyPath: "center.x", type: .tiltAlongHorizontalAxis)

horizontalMotionEffect.minimumRelativeValue = -10

horizontalMotionEffect.maximumRelativeValue = 10

myView.addMotionEffect(horizontalMotionEffect)
```

This code creates a horizontal parallax effect that responds to device tilting.

5. Interactive Animations

Interactive animations allow users to engage with your app's interface. You can use gestures and animations to create interactive elements. For example, you can implement swipe gestures to reveal hidden content or create draggable views.

```
let swipeGesture = UISwipeGestureRecognizer(target: self, action: #selector(handleSwipe))

myView.addGestureRecognizer(swipeGesture)

@objc func handleSwipe() {

// Implement animation here

}
```

In this example, when the user swipes the view, the handleSwipe function is called, allowing you to perform animations in response to the gesture.

By implementing these visual effects in your iOS app, you can enhance its aesthetics and user engagement. Experiment with different effects and combinations to create a visually stunning and interactive user interface. In the next section, we'll explore how to create custom transitions to further enhance your app's user experience.

Section 12.4: Creating Custom Transitions

Custom transitions in iOS apps allow you to add unique and engaging animations when transitioning between view controllers.

These animations can make your app stand out and provide a more immersive user experience. In this section, we'll explore how to create custom view controller transitions.

1. Custom Transition Delegates

To implement custom transitions, you'll need to conform to the UIViewControllerAnimatedTransitioning and UIViewControllerTransitioningDelegate protocols. Here's a basic structure of how you can create a custom transition delegate:

```
class CustomTransitionDelegate: NSObject, UIViewControllerTransitioningDelegate {

func animationController(forPresented presented: UIViewController, presenting: UIViewController, source: UIViewController) -> UIViewControllerAnimatedTransitioning?
{

return CustomPresentTransition()

}

func animationController(forDismissed dismissed: UIViewController) -> UIViewControllerAnimatedTransitioning?
{

return CustomDismissTransition()

}

}
```

In this example, we have a CustomTransitionDelegate class that provides transitions for presenting and dismissing view controllers.

We'll create the CustomPresentTransition and CustomDismissTransition classes to define the animations.

2. Animating Presentations

Let's create the CustomPresentTransition class. This class should conform to the UIViewControllerAnimatedTransitioning protocol and define the animation for presenting a view controller. Here's a simplified example:

```
class CustomPresentTransition: NSObject, UIViewControllerAnimatedTransitioning {

func transitionDuration(using transitionContext: UIViewControllerContextTransitioning?) -> TimeInterval {

return 0.5 // Animation duration

}

func animateTransition(using transitionContext: UIViewControllerContextTransitioning) {

guard let fromVC = transitionContext.viewController(forKey: .from),

let toVC = transitionContext.viewController(forKey: .to) else {

return

}

let containerView = transitionContext.containerView

containerView.addSubview(toVC.view)

// Implement your custom presentation animation here
```

```
toVC.view.alpha = 0.0

UIView.animate(withDuration: transitionDuration(using: transitionContext), animations: {

toVC.view.alpha = 1.0

}) { _ in

transitionContext.completeTransition(true)

}

}

}
```

In this example, we define a custom presentation animation by gradually fading in the toVC view controller.

3. Animating Dismissals

Now, let's create the CustomDismissTransition class, which defines the animation for dismissing a view controller:

```
class CustomDismissTransition: NSObject, UIViewControllerAnimatedTransitioning {

func transitionDuration(using transitionContext: UIViewControllerContextTransitioning?) -> TimeInterval {

return 0.5 // Animation duration

}

func animateTransition(using transitionContext: UIViewControllerContextTransitioning) {
```

```
guard let fromVC = transitionContext.viewController(forKey: .from),

let toVC = transitionContext.viewController(forKey: .to) else {

return

}

let containerView = transitionContext.containerView

// Implement your custom dismissal animation here

UIView.animate(withDuration: transitionDuration(using: transitionContext), animations: {

fromVC.view.alpha = 0.0

}) { _ in

transitionContext.completeTransition(true)

}

}

}
```

In this example, we define a custom dismissal animation by gradually fading out the fromVC view controller.

4. Setting Up the Custom Transition

To use the custom transition, you'll need to set the transitioning delegate of your presenting view controller and specify the modal presentation style as .custom. Here's how you can present a view controller with the custom transition:

```
let customTransitionDelegate = CustomTransitionDelegate()

presentedViewController.modalPresentationStyle = .custom

presentedViewController.transitioningDelegate = customTransitionDelegate

present(presentedViewController, animated: true, completion: nil)
```

With this setup, when you present or dismiss a view controller, the custom animations defined in the CustomPresentTransition and CustomDismissTransition classes will be triggered.

Custom transitions provide endless possibilities for creating visually appealing and interactive animations in your iOS app. You can customize these transitions further by modifying view properties, applying transformations, and more. Experiment with different animations to achieve the desired effects for your app's transitions.

Section 12.5: Enhancing User Interface with Animation

Animation is a powerful tool in enhancing the user interface (UI) of your iOS app. It can make your app feel more responsive, engaging, and visually appealing. In this section, we'll explore various techniques and best practices for enhancing the user interface with animation.

1. Subtle Feedback Animations

Subtle animations can provide feedback to users, making interactions feel more natural. For example, when a button is tapped, you can apply a slight scale or opacity animation to indicate the tap's recognition. Here's a basic example in Swift:

```
UIView.animate(withDuration: 0.2, animations: {
button.transform = CGAffineTransform(scaleX: 0.95, y: 0.95)
}) { _ in
UIView.animate(withDuration: 0.2) {
button.transform = .identity
}
}
```

This code scales down the button briefly when it's tapped and returns it to its original size.

2. Smooth Transitions

When transitioning between different views or screens, smooth animations can provide context and improve the user experience. Consider using custom transitions (as discussed in Section 12.4) for more complex transitions, such as sliding, fading, or zooming effects.

3. Feedback on Long-Running Tasks

If your app performs long-running tasks, like fetching data from a server, use activity indicators or progress bars to keep users informed. Animate these elements to indicate progress visually. For example, for a progress bar animation:

```
UIView.animate(withDuration: 0.5) {
progressBar.frame.size.width = progress * containerWidth
}
```

4. Parallax Effects

Parallax effects can create a sense of depth in your app's UI. You can implement parallax scrolling in UIScrollView or create custom parallax effects for specific UI elements. Here's a simple parallax effect for a UIImageView:

```
func applyParallaxEffect(to imageView: UIImageView) {

let horizontalEffect = UIInterpolatingMotionEffect(keyPath: "center.x", type: .tiltAlongHorizontalAxis)

horizontalEffect.minimumRelativeValue = -10

horizontalEffect.maximumRelativeValue = 10

let verticalEffect = UIInterpolatingMotionEffect(keyPath: "center.y", type: .tiltAlongVerticalAxis)

verticalEffect.minimumRelativeValue = -10

verticalEffect.maximumRelativeValue = 10

let group = UIMotionEffectGroup()

group.motionEffects = [horizontalEffect, verticalEffect]

imageView.addMotionEffect(group)

}
```

5. Dynamic Layout Changes

Animating changes in your UI layout can create a smoother experience when elements appear or disappear. For instance, when showing or hiding a view:

```
UIView.animate(withDuration: 0.3) {
```

```
viewToHide.alpha = 0.0

viewToShow.alpha = 1.0

self.view.layoutIfNeeded()

}
```

6. Gesture-Driven Animations

Allowing gestures, like swipe or pinch, to trigger animations can engage users and make your app more interactive. Consider using UIGestureRecognizer to detect gestures and initiate animations based on user input.

7. Test on Real Devices

When implementing animations, it's essential to test on real devices with varying performance capabilities. Ensure that animations run smoothly and do not negatively impact the app's responsiveness.

8. Combine Animations

Combine multiple animations to create complex effects. For instance, you can combine scale and rotation animations to give the impression of an element spinning and zooming simultaneously.

```
UIView.animate(withDuration: 1.0) {

view.transform = CGAffineTransform(rotationAngle: .pi).concatenating(CGAffineTransform(scaleX: 2.0, y: 2.0))

}
```

9. Performance Optimization

Keep animations lightweight to maintain good performance. Avoid excessive use of animations, especially on older devices. Profile your app to identify and optimize performance bottlenecks.

Enhancing the user interface with animations requires creativity and attention to detail. Consider the user's context and the overall user experience when implementing animations in your iOS app. Well-designed animations can make your app feel polished and delightful to use.

Chapter 13: Core Location and Maps

Location-based services are a fundamental part of many modern iOS applications. They enable apps to provide location-aware features, such as mapping, navigation, and location-based notifications. In this chapter, we will explore Core Location, Apple's framework for working with location data, and how to integrate maps into your iOS app.

Section 13.1: Location Services in iOS

Location services in iOS allow your app to determine the device's geographic location and orientation. This information can be used for a wide range of purposes, from providing turn-by-turn directions to tagging photos with location data.

Core Location Framework

The Core Location framework provides the necessary classes and APIs to interact with the device's GPS, cellular, and Wi-Fi hardware for location-related tasks. Here's an overview of some essential components:

1. **CLLocationManager**: This class manages the delivery of location data to your app. You create an instance of CLLocationManager to start and stop location updates.
2. **CLLocation**: The CLLocation class represents a geographic coordinate along with altitude and accuracy information. It's used to store location data.
3. **CLLocationCoordinate2D**: This is a C struct that defines a geographic coordinate as latitude and longitude.

Requesting Location Permissions

Before you can access a user's location, your app must request permission. iOS provides two levels of location access:

- **When In Use**: Your app can access location data while running in the foreground.

- **Always**: Your app can access location data even when running in the background.

To request permission, you need to add the appropriate key-value pairs to your app's Info.plist file, explaining why your app needs location data. You also need to request authorization using CLLocationManager.

```
let locationManager = CLLocationManager()

func requestLocationPermission() {

locationManager.delegate = self

locationManager.requestWhenInUseAuthorization() // or .requestAlwaysAuthorization()

}
```

Receiving Location Updates

To receive location updates, you need to implement the CLLocationManagerDelegate methods. The most important method is didUpdateLocations, which is called when new location data is available.

```
func locationManager(_ manager: CLLocationManager, didUpdateLocations locations: [CLLocation]) {

if let location = locations.last {

// Handle the new location data

}

}
```

Handling Location Errors

Location services may encounter errors, such as the user denying permission or the device's location hardware being unavailable. You should implement the locationManager(_:didFailWithError:) delegate method to handle such errors gracefully.

```
func locationManager(_ manager: CLLocationManager, didFailWithError error: Error) {

// Handle the error

}
```

Managing Location Updates

You can control the frequency and accuracy of location updates by configuring the CLLocationManager object. Set properties like desiredAccuracy and distanceFilter to suit your app's needs.

locationManager.desiredAccuracy = kCLLocationAccuracyNearestTenMeters

locationManager.distanceFilter = 10.0 // *Update only when the device moves at least 10 meters*

Location Simulation in Simulator

When testing location-based features in the iOS Simulator, you can simulate location changes using the "Features" menu. You can set a custom location or simulate movement along a predefined route.

In this section, we've covered the fundamentals of location services in iOS using Core Location. Next, we'll explore working with Core Location to access the device's location data programmatically and build location-aware features.

Section 13.2: Working with Core Location

Now that we have a basic understanding of location services in iOS using Core Location, let's dive deeper into working with this framework. We'll explore how to request and retrieve the device's location, geocoding, reverse geocoding, and monitoring significant location changes.

Requesting Location Updates

Once you've obtained the user's permission to access their location, you can start requesting location updates. Remember that you need to set the delegate for your CLLocationManager instance and request the appropriate authorization, as discussed in the previous section.

To initiate location updates, you can call the startUpdatingLocation() method on your CLLocationManager instance.

```
let locationManager = CLLocationManager()

func startLocationUpdates() {

locationManager.delegate = self

locationManager.startUpdatingLocation()

}
```

Location updates will be delivered to the didUpdateLocations delegate method, as explained earlier.

Geocoding and Reverse Geocoding

Geocoding is the process of converting a location's coordinates (latitude and longitude) into a human-readable address. Reverse geocoding, on the other hand, involves converting an address or place name into geographic coordinates.

Apple provides classes for both geocoding and reverse geocoding:

- **CLGeocoder**: This class is used for geocoding and reverse geocoding operations. You can create an instance of CLGeocoder and use its methods to convert between coordinates and addresses.

Geocoding Example

```
let geocoder = CLGeocoder()

func geocodeLocation(latitude: CLLocationDegrees, longitude: CLLocationDegrees) {

let location = CLLocation(latitude: latitude, longitude: longitude)

geocoder.reverseGeocodeLocation(location) { (placemarks, error) in

if let error = error {

// Handle the geocoding error

print("Geocoding error: \(error.localizedDescription)")

} else if let placemark = placemarks?.first {

// Access the placemark's address information

let address = placemark.compactAddress ?? "No address found"

print("Address: \(address)")

}

}

}
```

Reverse Geocoding Example

```
let geocoder = CLGeocoder()

func reverseGeocodeAddress(address: String) {

geocoder.geocodeAddressString(address) { (placemarks, error) in

if let error = error {

// Handle the reverse geocoding error

print("Reverse geocoding error: \(error.localizedDescription)")

} else if let placemark = placemarks?.first {

// Access the placemark's coordinates

let coordinates = placemark.location?.coordinate

print("Coordinates: \(coordinates?.latitude ?? 0), \(coordinates?.longitude ?? 0)")

}

}

}
```

Monitoring Significant Location Changes

In some cases, you may not need continuous, high-precision location updates. Instead, you can use significant location change monitoring to receive updates only when the device's location changes significantly, such as when it moves between cell towers.

```
func startMonitoringSignificantLocationChanges() {
```

```
locationManager.delegate = self

locationManager.startMonitoringSignificantLocationChanges()

}
```

Implement the didUpdateLocations delegate method as usual, and it will be called when significant location changes occur.

This section has provided an overview of working with Core Location in iOS, including requesting location updates, geocoding, reverse geocoding, and monitoring significant location changes. In the next section, we'll explore how to display maps and annotations in your iOS app using MapKit.

Section 13.3: Displaying Maps and Annotations

In this section, we'll delve into using MapKit, which allows you to display maps, annotations, and interactive map-based experiences in your iOS app. MapKit provides a high-level interface for integrating maps, making it easy to show locations, directions, and more.

Adding MapKit to Your Project

To get started with MapKit, you'll need to add it to your project. Open your Xcode project, go to the "File" menu, and select "Add Packages...". Search for "MapKit" and add it to your project. This will enable you to use MapKit in your app.

Creating a Map View

The central component of MapKit is the MKMapView class, which you can use to display maps in your app's user interface. You can add a map view either programmatically or using Interface Builder.

Programmatically Adding a Map View

Here's an example of how to add a map view to your view controller programmatically:

```
import UIKit

import MapKit

class MapViewController: UIViewController {

@IBOutlet weak var mapView: MKMapView!

override func viewDidLoad() {

super.viewDidLoad()

// Set the initial region for the map

let initialLocation = CLLocationCoordinate2D(latitude: 37.7749, longitude: -122.4194)

let region = MKCoordinateRegion(center: initialLocation, latitudinalMeters: 10000, longitudinalMeters: 10000)

mapView.setRegion(region, animated: true)

// Add an annotation to the map

let annotation = MKPointAnnotation()

annotation.coordinate = initialLocation

annotation.title = "San Francisco"

mapView.addAnnotation(annotation)

}
```

}

Using Interface Builder

To add a map view using Interface Builder, drag and drop a "Map View" object from the Object Library to your view controller's view. You can then connect the map view to your view controller by creating an outlet.

Adding Annotations

Annotations are used to mark specific locations on the map. You can customize the appearance of annotations by adopting the MKAnnotation protocol and creating your own annotation classes.

Here's a simple example of creating a custom annotation class:

```
import MapKit

class CustomAnnotation: NSObject, MKAnnotation {

var coordinate: CLLocationCoordinate2D

var title: String?

var subtitle: String?

init(coordinate: CLLocationCoordinate2D, title: String?, subtitle: String?) {

self.coordinate = coordinate

self.title = title

self.subtitle = subtitle

}
```

```
}
```

You can add your custom annotations to the map view using the addAnnotation method:

```
let annotation = CustomAnnotation(coordinate: CLLocationCoordinate2D(latitude: 37.7749, longitude: -122.4194), title: "San Francisco", subtitle: "The Golden City")

mapView.addAnnotation(annotation)
```

Customizing Annotations

MapKit provides a way to customize the appearance of annotations using MKAnnotationView. You can create a custom annotation view by subclassing MKAnnotationView and providing your own visuals, such as images or custom graphics.

```
import MapKit

class CustomAnnotationView: MKAnnotationView {

override init(annotation: MKAnnotation?, reuseIdentifier: String?)
{

super.init(annotation: annotation, reuseIdentifier: reuseIdentifier)

self.image = UIImage(named: "custom_pin")

}

required init?(coder aDecoder: NSCoder) {

super.init(coder: aDecoder)

}

}
```

To use your custom annotation view, set the MKMapViewDelegate and implement the viewFor delegate method:

```
func mapView(_ mapView: MKMapView, viewFor annotation: MKAnnotation) -> MKAnnotationView? {

if annotation is MKUserLocation {

return nil // Don't customize the user's location annotation

}

if let customAnnotation = annotation as? CustomAnnotation {

let annotationView = CustomAnnotationView(annotation: customAnnotation, reuseIdentifier: "customAnnotation")

return annotationView

}

return nil // Return nil for other annotations

}
```

This covers the basics of displaying maps and annotations using MapKit in your iOS app. You can further enhance your map-based features by integrating directions, overlays, and user interactions, which we'll explore in the next sections.

Section 13.4: Geofencing and Location-Based Apps

Geofencing is a powerful feature in iOS that allows you to define virtual boundaries around real-world geographic areas. You can use geofencing to trigger actions when a user enters or exits a defined region, such as sending notifications, changing app behavior, or logging location data. In this section, we'll explore geofencing and how to build location-based apps using Core Location and MapKit.

Core Location Framework

To work with geofencing and location-based features, you'll primarily use the Core Location framework. Core Location provides classes and services for accessing and monitoring the device's location and heading information.

Requesting Location Permissions

Before using Core Location, you must request the appropriate location permissions from the user. Depending on your app's requirements, you can request "When In Use" or "Always" location permissions. Add the necessary keys to your app's Info.plist file to describe why you need location access.

Here's an example of adding keys to your Info.plist:

- NSLocationWhenInUseUsageDescription: A message that explains why your app needs location access while in use.
- NSLocationAlwaysUsageDescription: A message that explains why your app needs background location access.

Getting the User's Location

You can use Core Location to retrieve the user's current location using the CLLocationManager class. Here's a basic example of how to set up and use CLLocationManager to get the user's location:

import CoreLocation

```
class LocationManager: NSObject, CLLocationManagerDelegate {

private let locationManager = CLLocationManager()

override init() {

super.init()

locationManager.delegate = self

locationManager.requestWhenInUseAuthorization() // Request "When In Use" location permission

locationManager.startUpdatingLocation()

}

func locationManager(_ manager: CLLocationManager, didUpdateLocations locations: [CLLocation]) {

if let location = locations.last {

// Use the user's location here

print("Latitude: \(location.coordinate.latitude), Longitude: \(location.coordinate.longitude)")

}

}

}
```

Geofencing with Core Location

To set up geofencing in your app, you can use the CLCircularRegion class, which defines a circular geographic region with a center coordinate and radius. You can create one or more regions and add them to your CLLocationManager for monitoring.

Here's a basic example of how to set up geofencing:

```
import CoreLocation

class GeofenceManager: NSObject, CLLocationManagerDelegate {

private let locationManager = CLLocationManager()

override init() {

super.init()

locationManager.delegate = self

locationManager.requestAlwaysAuthorization() // Request "Always" location permission for geofencing

}

func startMonitoringRegion(center: CLLocationCoordinate2D, radius: CLLocationDistance, identifier: String) {

let region = CLCircularRegion(center: center, radius: radius, identifier: identifier)

region.notifyOnEntry = true // Notify when the user enters the region

region.notifyOnExit = true // Notify when the user exits the region

locationManager.startMonitoring(for: region)

}

func locationManager(_ manager: CLLocationManager, didEnterRegion region: CLRegion) {
```

```
// Handle entering the geofence region
print("Entered geofence region: \(region.identifier)")
}
func locationManager(_ manager: CLLocationManager, didExitRegion region: CLRegion) {
// Handle exiting the geofence region
print("Exited geofence region: \(region.identifier)")
}
}
```

In this example, we create a GeofenceManager that uses CLLocationManager to monitor geofence regions. When the user enters or exits a region, the corresponding delegate methods are called.

Building Location-Based Apps

Geofencing opens up possibilities for location-based apps. You can use geofencing to create location-aware reminders, trigger notifications when users reach specific places, or customize app behavior based on a user's current location.

For example, you could build a location-based to-do list app that reminds users to buy groceries when they enter a supermarket or reminds them to pick up dry cleaning when they are near the dry cleaner's location.

Keep in mind that effective use of geofencing should always prioritize user privacy and request the appropriate location permissions while providing clear and transparent explanations for why location data is being collected.

In the next section, we'll explore privacy considerations when working with location-based features.

Section 13.5: Privacy Considerations for Location

Privacy is a fundamental concern when developing location-based apps that use Core Location and geofencing. Users expect their location data to be handled responsibly and securely. In this section, we'll explore key privacy considerations and best practices for location-based app development.

Requesting Minimal Location Permissions

To respect user privacy, it's essential to request only the minimum location permissions necessary for your app's functionality. iOS offers two main levels of location permission:

1. **When In Use**: This permission allows your app to access the user's location only while the app is in the foreground. Use this permission if your app's core functionality relies on real-time location data, such as navigation or fitness tracking.
2. **Always**: This permission allows your app to access the user's location both in the foreground and background. Request this permission if your app requires continuous location monitoring, such as geofencing or location-based notifications.

When you request location permissions, be clear in explaining why your app needs access to the user's location. In your app's Info.plist file, provide usage descriptions for both "When In Use" and "Always" location access. These descriptions should be concise and informative, detailing how the location data will improve the user's experience.

Educate Users on Privacy Settings

Empower users with control over their location data by providing easy access to privacy settings within your app. Offer a settings screen where users can review and change their location permissions. Additionally, include an explanation of the benefits of enabling location services and the impact on app functionality.

Here's an example of how you can guide users to location privacy settings within your app:

```
import UIKit

import CoreLocation

class LocationPrivacyViewController: UIViewController {

@IBOutlet weak var privacySettingsButton: UIButton!

@IBAction func openPrivacySettings(_ sender: Any) {

if let privacyURL = URL(string: UIApplication.openSettingsURLString) {

UIApplication.shared.open(privacyURL, options: [:], completionHandler: nil)

}

}

// ...
```

```
}
```

In this example, the openPrivacySettings function opens the device's settings app to the location privacy settings page when the user taps the "Privacy Settings" button.

Securely Store Location Data

If your app collects and stores location data, it's crucial to handle this data securely. Implement data encryption and follow best practices for data storage and transmission. Ensure that location data is anonymized and cannot be linked directly to individual users.

Periodic Location Reminders

For apps that use geofencing to send location-based reminders or notifications, consider offering options for users to set the frequency and time window for reminders. This allows users to control when and how often they receive location-based alerts, reducing potential annoyance.

Transparent Privacy Policy

Create and maintain a clear and concise privacy policy that outlines how your app collects, uses, and stores location data. Make this policy easily accessible within your app, especially during the onboarding process. Users should have a clear understanding of how their location data is being handled and protected.

User Consent and Opt-Out

Give users the ability to provide informed consent for location data collection and processing. Allow users to opt out of location services at any time, and respect their choice promptly. When users opt out, ensure that your app stops collecting and using their location data.

By following these best practices, you can develop location-based apps that not only provide valuable features but also prioritize user privacy and security. Respecting user privacy builds trust and encourages users to continue using your app.

Chapter 14: Notifications and Background Tasks

In Chapter 14, we delve into the critical aspects of notifications and background tasks in iOS app development. Notifications play a pivotal role in keeping users engaged with your app, while background tasks ensure that your app can perform essential operations even when it's not actively running.

Section 14.1: Local Notifications

Local notifications are a powerful tool for sending alerts, reminders, and updates to users directly from your app. These notifications are generated and delivered locally on the user's device, providing a seamless way to keep users informed.

Scheduling Local Notifications

To schedule a local notification, you'll need to use the UNUserNotificationCenter framework introduced in iOS 10. Here's an example of scheduling a simple local notification:

```
import UserNotifications

// Request permission to display notifications

UNUserNotificationCenter.current().requestAuthorization(options: [.alert, .sound, .badge]) { (granted, error) in
```

```
if granted {

// Create a notification content instance

let content = UNMutableNotificationContent()

content.title = "Your Reminder"

content.body = "Don't forget your meeting at 2 PM!"

// Create a notification trigger (e.g., a time-based trigger)

let date = Date().addingTimeInterval(60) // Notification after 60 seconds

let trigger = UNTimeIntervalNotificationTrigger(timeInterval: 60, repeats: false)

// Create a notification request

let request = UNNotificationRequest(identifier: "meetingReminder", content: content, trigger: trigger)

// Schedule the notification

UNUserNotificationCenter.current().add(request) { (error) in

if let error = error {

print("Error scheduling notification: \(error.localizedDescription)")

} else {

print("Notification scheduled successfully!")

}

}
```

```
}
}
```

In this code snippet:

- We request authorization from the user to display notifications with specific options (alert, sound, and badge).
- We create a UNMutableNotificationContent instance to define the notification's title and body.
- A notification trigger is set using UNTimeIntervalNotificationTrigger, which schedules the notification to fire after a specified time interval (in this case, 60 seconds).
- We create a UNNotificationRequest that includes the notification's content and trigger.
- Finally, we use UNUserNotificationCenter to schedule the notification.

Handling User Actions

Local notifications can also include action buttons that allow users to interact with the notification directly. For example, users can dismiss or open the app from the notification itself. Here's how you can handle user actions:

```
// Implement the UNUserNotificationCenterDelegate
class NotificationDelegate: NSObject, UNUserNotificationCenterDelegate {
```

```
// Called when a notification is delivered to a foreground app

func userNotificationCenter(_ center: UNUserNotificationCenter, willPresent notification: UNNotification, withCompletionHandler completionHandler: @escaping (UNNotificationPresentationOptions) -> Void) {

// Display the notification when the app is in the foreground

completionHandler([.banner, .sound])

}

// Called when a user taps on a notification or action button

func userNotificationCenter(_ center: UNUserNotificationCenter, didReceive response: UNNotificationResponse, withCompletionHandler completionHandler: @escaping () -> Void) {

// Handle the user's response here

completionHandler()

}

}

// Set the delegate

let notificationDelegate = NotificationDelegate()

UNUserNotificationCenter.current().delegate = notificationDelegate
```

In this code, we implement the UNUserNotificationCenterDelegate to handle notification-related events. The userNotificationCenter(_:willPresent:withCompletionHandler:)

method is called when a notification is delivered while the app is in the foreground, allowing you to specify how the notification should be presented to the user. The userNotificationCenter(_:didReceive:withCompletionHandler:) method is called when a user interacts with a notification.

Local notifications are a valuable tool for engaging users with your app and providing timely information. Whether it's reminding users of important events, notifying them of updates, or prompting them to take specific actions, mastering local notifications is crucial for enhancing the user experience.

In the following sections of this chapter, we'll explore more advanced notification techniques, including push notifications, background execution, and best practices for managing notifications in your iOS app.

Section 14.2: Push Notifications

Push notifications are a fundamental part of modern mobile app development, enabling you to send messages, updates, and alerts to users even when your app is not running. Unlike local notifications, push notifications are sent from a remote server to the user's device, allowing you to engage users with relevant information in real-time.

Configuring Push Notifications

To implement push notifications in your iOS app, you need to set up the necessary configurations in both your app and on your server. Here's a high-level overview of the process:

1. **Obtain an Apple Developer Account**: You must enroll in the Apple Developer Program and set up an App ID for your app.

2. **Create an APNs Key**: Generate an Apple Push Notification service (APNs) key, which is used to securely send notifications to Apple's servers.
3. **Configure App Permissions**: Request permission from the user to display notifications. You'll need to use the UserNotifications framework and request authorization.
4. **Register for Remote Notifications**: In your app's code, register for remote notifications using UIApplication.shared.registerForRemoteNotifications().
5. **Implement Push Notification Handling**: Implement methods to handle push notifications in your app delegate. For example, when a push notification is received, you can use the didReceiveRemoteNotification method to process it.

Here's an example of how to request notification permissions and register for remote notifications:

```
import UIKit

import UserNotifications

@UIApplicationMain

class AppDelegate: UIResponder, UIApplicationDelegate, UNUserNotificationCenterDelegate {

func application(_ application: UIApplication, didFinishLaunchingWithOptions launchOptions: [UIApplication.LaunchOptionsKey: Any]?) -> Bool {

// Request authorization to display notifications

UNUserNotificationCenter.current().requestAuthorization(options: [.alert, .sound, .badge]) { (granted, error) in
```

```
if granted {
DispatchQueue.main.async {
application.registerForRemoteNotifications()
}
} else if let error = error {
print("Error requesting authorization for notifications: \(error.localizedDescription)")
}
}
return true
}
func application(_ application: UIApplication, didRegisterForRemoteNotificationsWithDeviceToken deviceToken: Data) {
// Send the device token to your server for future notifications
let token = deviceToken.map { String(format: "%02.2hhx", $0) }.joined()
print("Device Token: \(token)")
}
func application(_ application: UIApplication, didFailToRegisterForRemoteNotificationsWithError error: Error) {
// Handle the error if registration fails
```

print("Failed to register for remote notifications: \(error.localizedDescription)")

}

// Handle push notifications when the app is in the foreground

func userNotificationCenter(_ center: UNUserNotificationCenter, willPresent notification: UNNotification, withCompletionHandler completionHandler: @escaping (UNNotificationPresentationOptions) -> Void) {

// Customize how the notification is presented when the app is in the foreground

completionHandler([.alert, .sound])

}

// Handle user interactions with push notifications

func userNotificationCenter(_ center: UNUserNotificationCenter, didReceive response: UNNotificationResponse, withCompletionHandler completionHandler: @escaping () -> Void) {

// Handle the user's response to the notification

completionHandler()

}

}

In this code:

• We request authorization to display notifications with specific options (alert, sound, and badge) using UNUserNotificationCenter.

• When the user grants permission, we register for remote notifications by calling application.registerForRemoteNotifications().

• The didRegisterForRemoteNotificationsWithDeviceToken method is called when registration is successful, and the device token is obtained. You should send this token to your server for future push notifications.

• If registration fails, the didFailToRegisterForRemoteNotificationsWithError method handles the error.

• We also implement the userNotificationCenter(_:willPresent:withCompletionHandler:) method to customize how push notifications are presented when the app is in the foreground.

• The userNotificationCenter(_:didReceive:withCompletionHandler:) method handles user interactions with push notifications.

Sending Push Notifications

To send push notifications to your app, you need a server-side component that communicates with the Apple Push Notification service (APNs). You can use various server-side technologies and tools to achieve this. When sending a push notification, you'll specify the target device using the device token obtained during registration.

```
// Example server-side code in Node.js using the 'apn' library

const apn = require('apn');

const options = {

token: {

key: 'your-apns-key.p8',

keyId: 'your-key-id',

teamId: 'your-team-id',

},

production: false, // Set to true for production environment

};

const apnProvider = new apn.Provider(options);

const deviceToken = 'device-token-goes-here';

const notification = new apn.Notification({

alert: 'Hello, World!',
```

##

Section 14.3: Background Execution

In iOS app development, background execution refers to the ability of an app to perform tasks or execute code even when it's not **in** the foreground. This capability **is** essential **for** various scenarios, such

as updating content, fetching data, and responding to push notifications, **while** ensuring a smooth user experience.

Types of Background Execution

iOS offers several background execution modes to cater to different app requirements. Here are some of the most common ones:

1. **Background Fetch**: This mode allows your app to periodically fetch data from a remote server **in** the background. iOS determines the optimal times **for** background fetch based on the app's usage patterns.

2. **Remote Notifications**: When your app receives a remote notification, it can execute code **in** the background to handle the notification, update content, or perform other tasks.

3. **Background Processing**: Apps can **continue** executing code **in** the background **for** tasks like downloading large files, processing data, or performing tasks initiated by the user before switching to another app.

4. **Background Location Updates**: Apps that require location information can receive periodic location updates **in** the background. This **is** useful **for** navigation, location-based services, and geofencing.

5. **Background Audio**: Apps playing audio content can **continue** to **do** so **in** the background, ensuring a seamless audio experience **while** users use other apps or lock their devices.

Implementing Background Execution

To enable background execution **in** your app, you need to configure specific capabilities and handle background events appropriately. Here's a general outline of the steps involved:

1. **Enable Background Modes**: In your Xcode project settings, navigate to the "Signing & Capabilities" tab and enable the necessary background modes based on your app's requirements. For example, if your app needs background fetch, enable the "Background Fetch" capability.

2. **Request Permission**: If your app needs to perform background tasks in response to remote notifications or location updates, you should request permission from the user to use these features. Implement the appropriate authorization requests using the relevant frameworks (e.g., `UNUserNotificationCenter` for notifications or `Core Location` for location updates).

3. **Handle Background Events**: Implement code in your app to handle background events. For instance, if your app receives a remote notification, you can respond to it in the `application(_:didReceiveRemoteNotification:fetchCompletionHandle method of your app delegate.

```swift
func application(_ application: UIApplication, didReceiveRemoteNotification userInfo: [AnyHashable : Any], fetchCompletionHandler completionHandler: @escaping (UIBackgroundFetchResult) -> Void) {

// Handle the remote notification and perform background tasks

// Call the completionHandler when tasks are complete

completionHandler(.newData)

}
```

1. **Optimize for Battery Life**: Be mindful of the resources

your app consumes in the background, such as CPU, network, and battery. Ensure efficient and responsible use of background execution to minimize the impact on the user's device.

2. **Testing**: Thoroughly test your app's background execution scenarios to ensure they work as expected and don't drain the device's battery excessively.

Background Execution Best Practices

While background execution is a powerful feature, it comes with responsibilities. Here are some best practices to follow:

- Use background execution modes only when necessary. Avoid enabling background modes that your app doesn't require, as they can negatively impact battery life and performance.

- Implement background tasks efficiently. Minimize the time your app spends in the background by completing tasks quickly and using background execution wisely.

- Handle errors gracefully. Be prepared for scenarios where background tasks might fail, and implement error handling and retry mechanisms as needed.

- Respect user privacy and permissions. Request user consent for background features like location updates and notifications, and explain why these features are essential for your app.

- Stay up-to-date with iOS updates. Apple may introduce changes to background execution rules and capabilities in iOS updates, so ensure your app remains compliant with the latest guidelines.

- Monitor battery usage. Keep an eye on your app's battery consumption, especially during background tasks, and optimize resource usage accordingly.

By following these best practices and understanding the different background execution modes, you can create iOS apps that provide a smooth and responsive user experience while efficiently utilizing background capabilities.

Section 14.4: Handling Background Tasks

In iOS app development, handling background tasks is crucial to ensure your app can perform work in the background efficiently and responsibly. Background tasks are tasks that continue to execute when your app is no longer in the foreground, allowing your app to remain responsive and provide a seamless user experience.

Types of Background Tasks

There are various types of background tasks, each suited to different scenarios. Here are some common types:

1. **Background Fetch**: Background fetch allows your app to periodically fetch data from a server, ensuring that your app always has up-to-date information when the user opens it. iOS determines the optimal times for background fetch based on the app's usage patterns.
2. **Background Processing**: This type of task is ideal for performing tasks like downloading large files, processing data, or performing tasks initiated by the user before switching to another app. Background processing helps

maintain app responsiveness.

3. **Background Location Updates**: Apps that rely on location information can receive periodic location updates even when in the background. This is valuable for navigation, location-based services, and geofencing.
4. **Background Audio**: Apps playing audio content can continue to do so in the background, ensuring a seamless audio experience while users use other apps or lock their devices.

Implementing Background Tasks

To implement background tasks effectively, follow these general steps:

1. **Enable Background Modes**: In Xcode, navigate to your project settings, go to the "Signing & Capabilities" tab, and enable the background modes relevant to your app's requirements. For instance, if your app needs background fetch, enable the "Background Fetch" capability.
2. **Request Permission**: If your app requires background tasks in response to remote notifications or location updates, request the necessary permissions from the user. Implement authorization requests using the relevant iOS frameworks.
3. **Handle Background Events**: Write code in your app to handle background events. For example, if your app receives a remote notification, respond to it in the application(_:didReceiveRemoteNotification:fetchCompletionH method of your app delegate.

```
func application(_ application: UIApplication, didReceiveRemoteNotification userInfo: [AnyHashable :
```

Any], fetchCompletionHandler completionHandler: @escaping (UIBackgroundFetchResult) -> Void) {

// Handle the remote notification and perform background tasks

// Call the completionHandler when tasks are complete

completionHandler(.newData)

}

1. **Optimize for Battery Life**: Be mindful of the resources your app consumes in the background, such as CPU, network, and battery. Ensure efficient and responsible use of background execution to minimize the impact on the user's device.
2. **Testing**: Thoroughly test your app's background execution scenarios to ensure they work as expected and don't excessively drain the device's battery.

Best Practices for Background Tasks

To make the most of background tasks and provide a great user experience, consider the following best practices:

- Enable background modes only when necessary. Avoid enabling background modes your app doesn't need, as they can negatively impact battery life and performance.

- Implement background tasks efficiently. Minimize the time your app spends in the background by completing tasks quickly and using background execution wisely.

- Handle errors gracefully. Be prepared for scenarios where background tasks might fail, and implement error handling and retry mechanisms as needed.

- Respect user privacy and permissions. Request user consent for background features like location updates and notifications, and explain why these features are essential for your app.

- Stay informed about iOS updates. Apple may introduce changes to background execution rules and capabilities in iOS updates, so ensure your app remains compliant with the latest guidelines.

- Monitor battery usage. Keep an eye on your app's battery consumption, especially during background tasks, and optimize resource usage accordingly.

By following these best practices and understanding the different types of background tasks available in iOS, you can create apps that provide a responsive and seamless user experience while efficiently utilizing background capabilities.

Section 14.5: Best Practices for App Notifications

Effective use of notifications can significantly enhance the user experience of your iOS app. Notifications keep users informed and engaged with your app's content and updates. However, it's crucial to use notifications judiciously and follow best practices to ensure they provide value to users rather than becoming a source of annoyance.

1. Relevance and Personalization

- **Targeted Content**: Send notifications that are relevant to the user's interests and app usage history. Personalization increases the likelihood of users engaging with notifications.

- **User Preferences**: Provide options in your app's settings to allow users to customize their notification preferences. Respect user choices regarding the types and frequency of notifications they receive.

2. Timing and Frequency

- **Scheduled Delivery**: Schedule notifications to be delivered at times when users are most likely to be active and receptive to your app's content. Avoid sending notifications during late hours.

- **Avoid Overloading**: Don't inundate users with a high frequency of notifications. Send only essential and timely updates to prevent users from disabling notifications for your app.

3. Clear and Informative Content

- **Concise Messages**: Keep notification messages concise and to the point. Users should be able to understand the purpose of the notification at a glance.

- **Actionable Content**: If applicable, make notifications actionable. Allow users to take specific actions directly from the notification, such as opening the app or responding to a message.

4. Design and Branding

- **Consistent Branding**: Maintain consistent branding in your notification content, including the use of your app's logo and colors. This helps users recognize your app's notifications.

- **Rich Media**: Use images, icons, or emojis to make notifications visually appealing and informative. Ensure that media files are appropriately sized for quick loading.

5. Notification Categories

- **Categorize Notifications**: Group notifications into categories to give users control over which types of notifications they receive. Allow users to opt in or out of specific categories.

6. Testing and Optimization

- **A/B Testing**: Experiment with different notification strategies using A/B testing to determine which approaches are most effective in engaging users.

- **Feedback Loop**: Collect and analyze user feedback regarding notifications. Use this feedback to refine your notification strategy over time.

7. Permissions and Privacy

- **Seek Permission**: Always request user permission to send notifications. Explain why notifications are essential and how they benefit the user.

- **Privacy Compliance**: Ensure that your notification practices comply with privacy regulations, such as the General Data Protection Regulation (GDPR) and the California Consumer Privacy Act (CCPA).

8. Opt-Out Mechanism

- **Unsubscribe Option**: Provide a clear and easy way for users to unsubscribe from notifications. This helps maintain a positive user experience.

9. Localization

- **Localized Content**: If your app is available in multiple languages, localize notification content to match the user's preferred language.

10. Monitoring and Analytics

- **Performance Tracking**: Monitor the performance of your notifications, including open rates and user engagement. Use analytics to assess the effectiveness of your notification campaigns.

- **Iterate and Improve**: Continuously iterate on your notification strategy based on performance data and user feedback.

By following these best practices, you can create a notification strategy that enhances user engagement, keeps users informed, and adds value to your iOS app. Effective notifications can contribute to user retention and satisfaction, ultimately benefiting your app's success.

Chapter 15: Debugging and Testing

Section 15.1: Debugging Techniques in Xcode

Debugging is an essential skill for any iOS developer. It's the process of identifying and fixing issues or bugs in your code. Xcode, Apple's integrated development environment, provides powerful tools and features to help you debug your iOS apps effectively. In this section, we'll explore some of the key debugging techniques and tools available in Xcode.

1. Setting Breakpoints

One of the fundamental debugging techniques is setting breakpoints in your code. A breakpoint is a marker that tells Xcode to pause program execution at a specific line of code. To set a breakpoint, simply click on the line number in the code editor's gutter. When your app runs and reaches that line, it will stop, allowing you to inspect variables, evaluate expressions, and step through the code.

2. Debug Area

Once your app stops at a breakpoint, you can use the Debug area in Xcode to inspect the current state of your app. The Debug area displays valuable information such as variable values, call stacks, and thread execution. You can also use the LLDB console to execute custom commands and view debugging output.

3. Stepping Through Code

Xcode provides several options for stepping through your code. The most common are:

- **Step Over (F6)**: This command advances the debugger to the next line of code in the current function, without entering into function calls.

- **Step Into (F7)**: Use this command to enter into a function or method call, allowing you to inspect the code within that function.

- **Step Out (F8)**: If you've stepped into a function and want to return to the calling function, use Step Out.

These stepping commands help you navigate through your code and understand how it executes.

4. Variables View

The Variables view in Xcode provides a convenient way to inspect the values of variables and objects at the current execution point. You can add variables of interest to this view by right-clicking and selecting "Add Expression." This allows you to track the state of specific variables as your app runs.

5. Exception Breakpoint

An Exception Breakpoint is a special type of breakpoint that pauses your app whenever an exception (runtime error) occurs. This is useful for catching and diagnosing unexpected issues in your code, such as nil value access or out-of-bounds array indexing.

6. View Hierarchy Debugger

For debugging issues related to your app's user interface, Xcode offers the View Hierarchy Debugger. This tool allows you to inspect the view hierarchy, including view controllers and their views, while your app is running. It can help you identify layout and rendering problems.

7. Memory Debugging

Memory-related issues, such as memory leaks and excessive memory usage, can be challenging to diagnose. Xcode includes tools like the Memory Graph Debugger and the Allocation Instrument to help you find and fix these problems. These tools provide insights into your app's memory usage and object references.

8. Breakpoint Actions

Breakpoints can have actions associated with them. For example, you can configure a breakpoint to print a message, log data, or even execute a custom script when the breakpoint is hit. This can be handy for automating debugging tasks.

In conclusion, mastering debugging techniques in Xcode is crucial for maintaining the quality and reliability of your iOS apps. These tools and practices empower you to identify and resolve issues efficiently, ensuring a smooth user experience.

Remember that debugging is not just about finding and fixing errors; it's also a valuable skill for understanding how your code works and improving your development skills.

Section 15.2: Profiling and Performance Optimization

Profiling and performance optimization are crucial aspects of iOS app development. Ensuring that your app runs smoothly and efficiently not only enhances the user experience but also prevents issues like crashes and excessive battery drain. In this section, we'll explore techniques and tools in Xcode for profiling and optimizing the performance of your iOS applications.

1. Instruments

Instruments is a powerful profiling tool bundled with Xcode that helps you analyze various aspects of your app's performance. You can access it through the "Product" menu by selecting "Profile." Instruments offers a wide range of predefined templates for profiling different aspects of your app, including:

- **Time Profiler**: Identifies performance bottlenecks by showing where your app spends the most time executing code.

- **Allocations**: Helps you monitor memory allocations and identify memory leaks.

- **Leaks**: Specifically focuses on finding memory leaks in your app.

- **Energy Impact**: Provides insights into how your app affects device battery life.

- **Network Connections**: Monitors network activity, including data usage and response times.

- **Core Data**: Analyzes Core Data interactions and database performance.

By running Instruments with the appropriate template, you can gather data on your app's behavior, pinpoint performance issues, and measure improvements as you optimize your code.

2. Time Profiler

The Time Profiler instrument is particularly useful for identifying performance bottlenecks in your code. It provides a graphical representation of CPU usage over time, making it easy to spot areas where your app is consuming excessive resources. To use Time Profiler:

1. Open Instruments and select the "Time Profiler" template.
2. Choose your target device or simulator and click the "Record" button.
3. Interact with your app to capture performance data.
4. After stopping the recording, you'll see a detailed timeline showing which functions consumed the most CPU time. Look for functions with significant self-times to identify potential optimization targets.

3. Leaks Instrument

The Leaks instrument is designed to detect memory leaks in your app. Memory leaks occur when objects are allocated but not deallocated, causing your app's memory footprint to grow over time. To use the Leaks instrument:

1. Open Instruments and select the "Leaks" template.
2. Choose your target device or simulator and click the "Record" button.
3. Interact with your app to simulate typical usage.
4. The Leaks instrument will identify any memory leaks and provide details about the leaked objects and their call stacks.

4. Energy Impact

Understanding how your app affects device battery life is crucial for delivering a positive user experience. The Energy Impact instrument helps you monitor energy consumption. To use it:

1. Open Instruments and select the "Energy Impact" template.
2. Choose your target device or simulator and click the "Record" button.
3. Use your app as you normally would.
4. The Energy Impact instrument will show a graph of your app's energy impact, including energy-efficient and energy-intensive periods.

5. Allocations Instrument

The Allocations instrument helps you track memory allocations and deallocations in your app. It's useful for identifying excessive memory usage and optimizing memory management. To use the Allocations instrument:

1. Open Instruments and select the "Allocations" template.
2. Choose your target device or simulator and click the "Record" button.
3. Exercise your app's functionality to capture memory allocation data.
4. You can inspect memory allocation events, including call stacks and object lifetimes, to identify areas for improvement.

In conclusion, profiling and performance optimization are integral parts of iOS app development. Xcode's Instruments toolset provides valuable insights into your app's behavior and performance. By using these tools, you can identify bottlenecks, memory leaks, and energy inefficiencies, ultimately delivering a smoother and more efficient app to your users. Regular profiling and optimization should be part of your development process to ensure the best possible user experience.

Section 15.3: Unit Testing in Swift

Unit testing is a fundamental practice in software development, including iOS app development. It involves testing individual units or components of your code to ensure they work as expected. In Swift, unit testing is supported through the XCTest framework, which is integrated into Xcode. In this section, we'll explore the importance of unit testing and how to write and run unit tests in Swift.

The Importance of Unit Testing

Unit testing serves several crucial purposes in iOS development:

1. **Early Detection of Bugs**: Unit tests help you catch and fix bugs during development, reducing the likelihood of shipping a flawed app to users.
2. **Code Documentation**: Tests act as documentation for your code. By writing tests, you define how your code should behave, which can be a valuable reference for both you and other developers.
3. **Regression Testing**: As your app evolves, unit tests provide a safety net, ensuring that existing functionality doesn't break when you make changes or additions to the codebase.
4. **Enhanced Refactoring**: When you refactor your code, unit tests can confirm that your changes haven't introduced

new bugs.

Writing Unit Tests in XCTest

To write unit tests in Swift, follow these steps:

1. **Create a Test Target**: In Xcode, add a unit test target to your project by selecting "File" > "New" > "Target..." and choosing "Unit Testing Bundle." This target will contain your test cases.
2. **Write Test Methods**: Create test methods within your test case classes. Test methods must start with the word "test" and should test specific aspects of your code.

```
import XCTest

@testable import YourApp // Import the module you want to test

class YourClassTests: XCTestCase {

func testAddition() {

let result = YourClass.add(2, 3)

XCTAssertEqual(result, 5, "Addition should return 5")

}

}
```

1. **Use XCTest Assertions**: XCTest provides various assertions, such as XCTAssertEqual, XCTAssertTrue, and XCTAssertFalse, to validate your code's behavior. These assertions compare actual results with expected results.
2. **Run Tests**: To run your tests, select your test target and

click the "Run" button in Xcode. Xcode will execute your tests and provide a summary of the results.

Test Coverage

Test coverage measures how much of your code is exercised by unit tests. Xcode provides a code coverage feature that highlights the lines of code covered by your tests. To view code coverage:

1. In Xcode, go to the "Product" menu, select "Scheme," and choose "Edit Scheme."
2. Under the "Test" section, enable "Gather coverage data."
3. Run your tests, and after completion, you can view code coverage by going to the "Report Navigator" and selecting the coverage report.

High test coverage indicates that your tests are thorough and that most of your code is validated. However, it's essential to focus on testing critical parts of your app thoroughly.

Best Practices

Here are some best practices for unit testing in Swift:

- Keep tests independent of each other.
- Write tests for boundary conditions and edge cases.
- Refactor and maintain your tests as your code evolves.
- Use setUp() and tearDown() methods to set up and tear down common resources for your test cases.
- Aim for a balance between test coverage and test quality.

Incorporating unit testing into your iOS development workflow can significantly improve code quality, reduce the number of bugs, and make your codebase more maintainable. It's a practice that professional iOS developers should embrace to build robust and reliable apps.

Section 15.4: UI Testing and Test Automation

UI testing is an essential part of iOS app development that goes beyond unit testing. While unit testing focuses on testing individual units of code, UI testing verifies the behavior and interactions of the app's user interface (UI) components. This section explores UI testing in iOS using the XCTest framework and Xcode's UI testing tools.

The Importance of UI Testing

UI testing ensures that your app's interface functions correctly and looks as expected. It allows you to automate interactions with your app's UI, simulating user actions like taps, swipes, and text input. UI testing is crucial for several reasons:

1. **End-to-End Testing**: UI tests simulate real user interactions, making them valuable for end-to-end testing to validate the entire user flow.
2. **Regression Testing**: As your app evolves, UI tests help ensure that new features or changes haven't introduced UI bugs.
3. **Consistency**: UI tests help maintain a consistent UI experience across different iOS device models and screen sizes.
4. **Localization**: UI tests can verify that your app's UI

elements display correctly in different languages and regions.

Writing UI Tests in XCTest

To write UI tests in XCTest, follow these steps:

1. **Create a UI Test Target**: In Xcode, add a UI test target to your project by selecting "File" > "New" > "Target..." and choosing "UI Testing Bundle." This target will contain your UI test cases.
2. **Record UI Interactions**: Xcode provides a recording feature that allows you to interact with your app's UI while it records your actions. To record UI interactions:

– Select your UI test target.

– Click the red record button in the Xcode UI testing pane.

– Interact with your app in the simulator or on a physical device.

Xcode will generate Swift code based on your interactions.

1. **Edit and Enhance Tests**: After recording, you can edit and enhance your UI test code. This might include adding assertions to verify expected UI states or interactions.

```
func testLogin() {

let app = XCUIApplication()

app.launch()
```

```
let usernameTextField = app.textFields["Username"]

usernameTextField.tap()

usernameTextField.typeText("yourusername")

let passwordTextField =
app.secureTextFields["Password"]

passwordTextField.tap()

passwordTextField.typeText("yourpassword")

app.buttons["Login"].tap()

XCTAssertTrue(app.staticTexts["Welcome"].exists,
"Login was not successful")

}
```

1. **Run UI Tests**: To run your UI tests, select your UI test target and click the "Run" button in Xcode. Xcode will launch the app in a simulator or on a physical device and execute the UI tests.

Test Automation

UI test automation is crucial for running tests consistently and efficiently. You can automate UI testing with continuous integration (CI) systems, such as Jenkins, Travis CI, or GitLab CI/CD. These systems can run your UI tests automatically whenever code changes are pushed to a repository.

Additionally, you can use tools like Fastlane or Firebase Test Lab to automate UI tests on real physical devices and a variety of simulators to ensure your app functions correctly on different iOS versions and devices.

Best Practices

Here are some best practices for UI testing in iOS:

- **Keep Tests Simple**: Break down complex UI tests into smaller, focused tests to make them more manageable and maintainable.
- **Use Page Objects**: Consider using the Page Object pattern to encapsulate interactions with different screens or view controllers in your app.
- **Parameterize Tests**: Make use of data-driven testing to run the same test with multiple sets of data to cover various scenarios.
- **Mock External Dependencies**: When necessary, mock external dependencies like network requests to isolate UI tests.

UI testing is an essential aspect of iOS app development that ensures your app's interface works as expected across different devices and scenarios. By incorporating UI testing into your development workflow, you can improve the quality and reliability of your iOS apps.

Section 15.5: Ensuring App Quality and Reliability

Ensuring the quality and reliability of your iOS app is a fundamental aspect of the development process. Users expect apps that are not only functional but also perform well and are free of bugs and crashes. In this section, we'll explore strategies and best practices for guaranteeing the quality and reliability of your iOS app.

1. Unit Testing and Test Coverage

Unit testing is the practice of testing individual units or components of your code in isolation. XCTest, the built-in testing framework in Xcode, provides a robust foundation for writing unit tests in Swift. Ensure good test coverage by writing tests for critical code paths and edge cases. Tools like Xcode's code coverage reports can help you identify untested code.

```
func testAddition() {

XCTAssertEqual(MathUtility.add(2, 3), 5, "Addition is incorrect")

}
```

2. Integration Testing

Integration testing focuses on verifying that different components of your app work correctly when combined. It ensures that your app's various parts interact seamlessly. XCTest can also be used for integration testing, but you may need to set up more complex test environments.

3. Continuous Integration (CI)

Implementing CI pipelines is crucial for automating the testing process. Services like Jenkins, Travis CI, or GitHub Actions can be used to automatically build, test, and distribute your app whenever code changes are pushed to your repository. CI ensures that tests are run consistently, preventing regressions.

4. Performance Testing

Performance is a critical aspect of app quality. Use Xcode's performance testing features to identify and address bottlenecks and memory issues. Instruments, a profiling tool included with Xcode, helps analyze your app's performance in detail.

5. Crash Reporting

Integrate a crash reporting tool like Crashlytics or Sentry to track and diagnose app crashes in real-time. Detailed crash reports can help you quickly identify the root causes of crashes and prioritize bug fixes.

6. Beta Testing

Leverage beta testing platforms like TestFlight to distribute pre-release versions of your app to a group of trusted testers. Their feedback can uncover issues that might not be apparent during internal testing.

7. User Acceptance Testing (UAT)

Conduct UAT with a select group of end-users to gather feedback on usability and user experience. Real users can provide valuable insights into how your app performs in real-world scenarios.

8. Automated UI Testing

Automate UI testing using XCTest and Xcode's UI testing tools to ensure that your app's UI components function correctly. UI tests simulate user interactions and help detect visual regressions.

9. Code Reviews

Implement a code review process to ensure code quality and identify potential issues early. Peer reviews help catch coding errors, improve code maintainability, and ensure adherence to coding standards.

10. Security Auditing

Regularly audit your app for security vulnerabilities. Be mindful of data protection, secure communication, and best practices for handling sensitive user information.

11. Documentation

Maintain clear and up-to-date documentation for your codebase. Documentation helps team members understand your code and its purpose, facilitating collaboration and maintenance.

12. Version Control

Use a version control system like Git to track changes to your codebase. Proper version control allows you to roll back to previous states and maintain a history of code changes.

13. Error Monitoring

Implement error monitoring tools like Sentry or Raygun to track and analyze non-fatal errors and exceptions. Monitoring errors helps you address issues proactively.

14. Performance Monitoring

Use performance monitoring tools like New Relic or Firebase Performance Monitoring to track app performance in production. Monitoring helps you identify and resolve performance bottlenecks.

15. User Feedback

Encourage users to provide feedback and bug reports through in-app mechanisms. User feedback can uncover issues specific to certain device configurations or usage patterns.

16. Regression Testing

After each update or new feature release, perform regression testing to ensure that existing functionality is not negatively impacted.

By incorporating these strategies and best practices into your iOS app development process, you can enhance the quality, reliability, and overall user satisfaction of your app. Building a robust and well-tested app is essential for long-term success in the competitive iOS app market.

Chapter 16: App Distribution and Deployment

Section 16.1: Preparing Your App for Submission

Preparing your iOS app for submission to the App Store is a crucial step in the app development process. This section will guide you through the steps required to ensure your app meets Apple's guidelines and is ready for distribution to users worldwide.

1. Code Review and Cleanup

Before submitting your app, conduct a thorough code review. Look for any unused or deprecated code, fix compiler warnings and errors, and ensure your code adheres to Swift and Apple's coding conventions. A clean and organized codebase makes maintenance and future updates easier.

2. Testing and Debugging

Test your app thoroughly on a variety of devices and iOS versions to identify and resolve any bugs or issues. Pay close attention to edge cases, such as low-memory scenarios and slow network conditions. Use the Xcode debugging tools to address any runtime issues.

3. App Icon and Launch Screen

Ensure your app has an appealing and correctly sized app icon. Additionally, create a launch screen that provides a smooth transition from the app launch to the main interface. Verify that the launch screen displays correctly on all devices and orientations.

4. App Store Screenshots and Previews

Create high-quality screenshots and preview videos that showcase your app's features and user interface. These visuals are crucial for attracting users on the App Store. Follow Apple's guidelines for screenshot sizes and formats.

5. App Store Metadata

Write compelling and accurate descriptions, keywords, and metadata for your app on the App Store Connect platform. Use relevant keywords to improve discoverability, and make sure your app's description and features are clear and concise.

6. Privacy Policy

If your app collects user data, ensure you have a privacy policy in place and provide a link to it on the App Store. Transparency about data usage is essential to build trust with users.

7. In-App Purchases and Subscriptions

If your app offers in-app purchases or subscriptions, set them up correctly on App Store Connect. Verify that purchase flows work as expected, and provide clear pricing information and terms to users.

8. App Store Guidelines Compliance

Review and adhere to Apple's App Store Review Guidelines. Ensure your app does not violate any of these guidelines, as non-compliance can result in rejection or removal from the App Store.

9. App Store Connect Configuration

Set up your app's details, pricing, availability, and release options on App Store Connect. Choose the countries and regions where your app will be available and configure pricing tiers.

10. App Store Review and Submission

Submit your app for review on App Store Connect. Apple's review process typically takes a few days, during which Apple checks your app for compliance with guidelines and policies. Be prepared to provide any additional information or documentation if requested.

11. App Store Optimization (ASO)

After your app is live on the App Store, focus on ASO strategies to improve its discoverability. Monitor user reviews and feedback to make ongoing improvements.

12. App Versioning and Updates

As you continue to develop your app, release updates with new features, bug fixes, and performance improvements. Keep your app's versioning consistent and maintain good communication with your user base.

13. Marketing and Promotion

Develop a marketing strategy to promote your app. Use social media, email marketing, and other channels to reach your target audience. Encourage users to leave positive reviews on the App Store.

14. App Analytics

Leverage App Store Connect and third-party analytics tools to track user engagement, retention, and other key metrics. Use this data to make data-driven decisions for future updates.

By following these steps, you can ensure that your iOS app is well-prepared for submission to the App Store. The process requires attention to detail, compliance with guidelines, and ongoing maintenance and improvement efforts to achieve success in the competitive app marketplace.

Section 16.2: App Store Connect and App Submission

Once you have prepared your iOS app for submission, the next step is to use App Store Connect, Apple's platform for managing and distributing your apps on the App Store. In this section, we'll explore the process of using App Store Connect to submit your app for review and eventual distribution.

1. Accessing App Store Connect

To begin, log in to App Store Connect using your Apple Developer account credentials. If you're part of a development team, make sure you have the necessary permissions to submit apps.

2. Adding Your App

Before you can submit your app, you need to add it to App Store Connect. Click on the "+ App" button and follow the prompts to provide details about your app, such as its name, bundle ID, and SKU. You'll also need to set up app-specific information, including the app's privacy policy URL, support URL, and marketing URL.

3. App Versions and Builds

For each version of your app, you'll create a new version record in App Store Connect. You'll also associate a specific build of your app with each version. Make sure you've built and archived your app using Xcode and have the necessary provisioning profiles in place.

4. App Store Information

Provide essential information about your app, such as its category, primary and secondary languages, and a detailed description. This information will be visible to users on the App Store.

5. Pricing and Availability

Set the price of your app or choose to offer it for free. Configure the availability of your app by selecting the countries and regions where you want it to be accessible. You can also specify release dates and pricing tiers for different markets.

6. App Previews and Screenshots

Upload high-quality screenshots and preview videos that showcase your app's features. Ensure they meet Apple's guidelines for resolution and format. These visuals play a crucial role in attracting users on the App Store.

7. App Review Information

Provide information that will help Apple's app review team understand your app's functionality and how to test it. Include any necessary login credentials or special instructions if your app requires them for testing.

8. App Store Review Submission

Once you've completed all the required information, you can submit your app for review. Apple's review process typically takes a few days, during which they check your app for compliance with guidelines and policies.

9. App Review Status

You can check the status of your app review in App Store Connect. Apple may approve your app, request changes, or, in some cases, reject it. Be prepared to provide any additional information or make necessary adjustments if required.

10. App Release and Distribution

If your app passes the review process, you can choose when to release it on the App Store. You can also use features like pre-orders to build excitement before the official launch.

11. Monitoring App Performance

After your app is live, use App Store Connect to monitor its performance. Track downloads, sales, user reviews, and other metrics. This data will help you make informed decisions about future updates and marketing strategies.

12. App Updates

As you continue to develop your app, release updates with new features, bug fixes, and improvements. Keep the versioning consistent and communicate with your users about changes.

13. App Store Optimization (ASO)

Optimize your app's visibility on the App Store by continuously refining keywords, descriptions, and visuals. Pay attention to user feedback and reviews to make ongoing improvements.

14. App Store Resources

Explore the wealth of resources available on the Apple Developer website and App Store Connect's help section. Apple provides detailed guidelines, best practices, and support for app developers.

By mastering the use of App Store Connect and following these steps, you can successfully submit your iOS app to the App Store, manage its distribution, and gather valuable insights into its performance. Remember that the app submission process is ongoing, and regular updates and improvements are essential for app success.

Section 16.3: Managing App Versions and Updates

One of the key aspects of maintaining a successful app on the App Store is managing app versions and updates effectively. In this section, we'll delve into the process of handling new versions, updates, and improvements for your iOS app.

1. Versioning Your App

Every release of your app should have a unique version number. Version numbers typically follow a format like "1.0," "1.1," "2.0," and so on. Use semantic versioning to communicate changes clearly to users and other developers. Increment the version number based on the significance of the changes:

- **Major Version (X.0.0):** Signifies significant changes or major updates that may introduce breaking changes or new features.

- **Minor Version (X.Y.0):** Indicates minor updates, including new features or improvements that are backward-compatible.

- **Patch Version (X.Y.Z):** Reserved for bug fixes and minor improvements that don't affect existing functionality.

2. Updating App Information

When you release a new version of your app, ensure that you update the app's information in App Store Connect. This includes revising the app's description, screenshots, and preview videos to reflect any new features or changes. App Store visitors should have accurate information about what to expect.

3. Release Notes

Writing detailed release notes is crucial. Users appreciate knowing what's new, what's been fixed, and what's improved in an update. This information can help increase user satisfaction and encourage them to keep your app updated.

4. Testing Updates

Before submitting an update to the App Store, thoroughly test your app to ensure that the changes and improvements work as intended. Check for any regressions and address any issues that arise during testing. Beta testing can be beneficial for getting user feedback on updates.

5. Version Compatibility

Consider version compatibility when making updates. Ensure that new versions of your app can handle data and settings from older versions gracefully. Implement migration or update logic if necessary.

6. App Store Review Process

When you submit an app update, it goes through the same review process as the initial app submission. Apple's review team checks for compliance with guidelines and policies, so ensure your update adheres to these standards.

7. Updating Rejected Apps

In some cases, an update may be rejected by the App Store review team. If this happens, carefully review the feedback provided by Apple and make the necessary changes to address the issues. You can then resubmit the updated version for review.

8. Timely Updates

Keep a regular schedule for updates to your app. Timely updates demonstrate your commitment to the app's ongoing development and improve user trust. Address critical issues promptly.

9. App Promotion

Promote your app updates to your user base. Use in-app notifications, email newsletters, and social media to inform users about the latest features and improvements. Encourage them to update to the latest version.

10. User Feedback

Pay attention to user feedback and reviews. User suggestions and bug reports can help guide your update priorities. Engage with your user community to understand their needs and expectations.

11. App Store Optimization (ASO)

Continue to optimize your app's presence on the App Store. Regularly refine keywords, descriptions, and visuals to maximize discoverability and appeal to potential users.

12. Measuring Update Impact

Use analytics tools to measure the impact of your updates. Track user engagement, retention, and any changes in user behavior. This data can inform your future development efforts.

13. Maintaining Compatibility

As iOS evolves and new devices are released, ensure that your app remains compatible with the latest operating system versions and device sizes. Regularly update dependencies and libraries.

14. Security Updates

Prioritize security updates and respond quickly to any security vulnerabilities that may arise. Users trust apps that take their security seriously.

By following these best practices for managing app versions and updates, you can maintain a healthy and engaging presence on the App Store. Consistent updates, clear communication with users, and attention to detail are key to ensuring your app's long-term success.

Section 16.4: App Distribution Methods

Once you've developed and tested your iOS app, the next step is distributing it to your target audience. There are several methods available for distributing iOS apps, each with its own use cases and considerations. In this section, we'll explore these distribution methods.

1. App Store Distribution

- **App Store:** This is the primary distribution method for consumer-facing apps. Submit your app to the App Store, where it undergoes a review process by Apple before becoming publicly available. Users can discover, download, and install your app from the App Store.

2. Ad Hoc Distribution

- **Ad Hoc Distribution:** This method is suitable for distributing your app to a limited number of devices, typically for testing or internal purposes. You can create an Ad Hoc distribution provisioning profile in Apple Developer Center and distribute the app via email or a secure download link. Users' devices must be registered in the provisioning profile.

3. Enterprise Distribution

- **Enterprise Distribution:** App distribution for organizations or enterprises allows them to deploy apps to their employees' devices without going through the App Store. It requires an Apple Enterprise Developer Program membership. Apps are distributed via a private server or mobile device management (MDM) solution.

4. TestFlight

- **TestFlight:** TestFlight is Apple's beta testing platform. It allows you to distribute pre-release versions of your app to a limited group of external testers. Users can install beta versions via the TestFlight app, providing valuable feedback before the official release.

5. In-House Distribution

- **In-House Distribution:** This method is similar to enterprise distribution but is intended for in-house apps within an organization. Apps are distributed to employees without the need for an App Store review. Requires an Apple Developer Enterprise Program membership.

6. Catalyst Distribution

- **Catalyst Distribution:** If you have a Mac Catalyst app, you can distribute it through the Mac App Store. Mac Catalyst allows you to bring your iPad app to the Mac platform, and distribution follows Mac App Store guidelines.

7. Custom Distribution Methods

- **Custom Distribution:** In some cases, you may require a custom distribution method. For example, for internal tools, you might use an internal server or third-party tools for distribution.

8. App Store Connect Configuration

- **App Store Connect:** Regardless of the distribution method, you'll need to configure your app in App Store Connect. This includes setting pricing, providing app metadata, and managing distribution settings.

9. User Engagement

- **User Engagement:** Regardless of the distribution method, actively engage with your users. Use app analytics to understand user behavior and preferences. Solicit feedback and iterate on your app to provide a better user experience.

10. App Updates

- **App Updates:** After your initial app distribution, continue to release updates with new features, bug fixes, and improvements. Frequent updates show your commitment to maintaining and enhancing your app.

11. Monitoring and Support

- **Monitoring and Support:** Be prepared to provide support to users. Monitor reviews and feedback in the App Store and other distribution channels. Address issues promptly and professionally.

12. Legal and Privacy Considerations

- **Legal and Privacy:** Ensure that your app complies with legal requirements and privacy regulations, such as

GDPR or COPPA. Protect user data and provide clear privacy policies.

13. Localization

- **Localization:** Consider localizing your app to reach a global audience. Translate app content and adapt it to different languages and regions.

14. App Marketing

- **App Marketing:** Promote your app to increase visibility and downloads. Use marketing strategies, including app store optimization (ASO), social media, and paid advertising, to attract users.

Choosing the right distribution method depends on your app's purpose, target audience, and business model. Understanding these options and effectively managing the distribution process is essential for the success of your iOS app.

Section 16.5: App Store Optimization Strategies

App Store Optimization (ASO) is the practice of improving your app's visibility and discoverability within app stores, such as the Apple App Store. ASO plays a crucial role in driving organic downloads and increasing your app's visibility among potential users. In this section, we'll explore various ASO strategies to help your iOS app succeed.

1. Keyword Research

- **Relevant Keywords:** Identify relevant keywords and phrases that potential users might use to search for apps like yours. Use tools and platforms that provide insights into popular and trending keywords.

- **Competitor Analysis:** Study the keywords used by your competitors and analyze their app descriptions. This can help you discover additional keywords to target.

- **Long-Tail Keywords:** Consider using long-tail keywords that are more specific to your app's niche. They may have less competition and can attract highly targeted users.

2. Optimize App Title and Subtitle

- **App Title:** Your app's title should include the primary keyword that best describes your app's core functionality. Keep it concise and memorable.

- **Subtitle:** The subtitle is an opportunity to provide additional context about your app. Use relevant keywords and highlight unique selling points (USPs) here.

3. App Description

- **Compelling Description:** Write a clear and engaging app description. Describe your app's features, benefits, and how it can solve users' problems.

• **Keyword Placement:** Integrate relevant keywords naturally within your app description to improve search visibility. Avoid keyword stuffing.

4. High-Quality App Icon and Screenshots

• **App Icon:** Your app icon is the first thing users see. Ensure it is visually appealing, reflects your brand, and stands out on the App Store.

• **Screenshots and Videos:** Include high-quality screenshots and, if applicable, a promotional video. Showcase your app's key features and user interface.

5. Ratings and Reviews

• **Encourage Reviews:** Encourage users to leave positive reviews and ratings. Prompt satisfied users to rate your app within the app.

• **Respond to Reviews:** Engage with users by responding to reviews, both positive and negative. Address concerns and show that you value feedback.

6. App Updates

• **Regular Updates:** Consistently release updates that improve your app's performance and add new features. Frequent updates can increase user engagement.

7. App Localization

- **Localized Metadata:** Localize your app's metadata, including the app title, subtitle, and description, to reach a broader international audience.

8. A/B Testing

- **Experimentation:** Conduct A/B tests with different versions of your app's title, icon, screenshots, and description to identify what resonates best with users.

9. App Store Advertising

- **Paid Advertising:** Consider using paid advertising within the App Store to promote your app. This includes Apple Search Ads, which allow you to bid on keywords.

10. Track and Analyze

- **Analytics:** Use app analytics tools to track user behavior, downloads, and conversion rates. Continuously analyze data to make informed ASO decisions.

11. App Previews

- **App Previews:** Create short app preview videos that demonstrate your app's key features. These can be featured on your App Store listing.

12. Optimize for Conversions

- **Conversion Rate Optimization (CRO):** Focus on optimizing your app's listing for conversions. Ensure that users who visit your page are more likely to download the app.

13. User Engagement and Retention

- **Retain Users:** Focus on retaining users by providing a great user experience. High retention rates positively impact your app's rankings.

14. External Promotion

- **External Promotion:** Promote your app on your website, social media, and other marketing channels to drive traffic to your App Store listing.

App Store Optimization is an ongoing process. Regularly review and update your ASO strategies to adapt to changes in user behavior, app store algorithms, and competitor landscape. By implementing these strategies effectively, you can increase your app's visibility, attract more users, and ultimately achieve greater success on the Apple App Store.

Chapter 17: Monetization and In-App Purchases

Section 17.1: Monetization Strategies for Apps

Monetization is a critical aspect of app development, as it allows developers to generate revenue from their hard work. In this section, we'll explore various monetization strategies that you can consider for your iOS app.

1. Freemium Model

- **Definition:** Under the freemium model, you offer your app for free with limited features or content. Users can unlock premium features or content through in-app purchases (IAPs).

- **Benefits:** This model attracts a large user base initially and encourages users to make IAPs to enhance their experience.

- **Examples:** Games often use this model to offer additional levels, power-ups, or virtual items for purchase.

2. Paid Apps

- **Definition:** In this straightforward model, users pay an upfront fee to download and use your app. There are no additional in-app purchases.

- **Benefits:** You generate revenue with each download. This model works well for apps with a strong value proposition.

- **Examples:** Productivity apps, professional tools, and some games use the paid app model.

3. Subscription Model

- **Definition:** Under the subscription model, users pay a recurring fee (e.g., monthly or annually) to access your app's premium features or content.

- **Benefits:** This model offers a predictable revenue stream and is suitable for apps that provide ongoing value.

- **Examples:** Streaming media services, news apps, and productivity tools commonly use subscriptions.

4. Ads and Ad Revenue

- **Definition:** You can monetize your app by displaying advertisements to users. Revenue is generated based on user interactions with ads.

- **Benefits:** This model can be effective for free apps and games, as it doesn't require direct payments from users.

- **Examples:** Many free apps and games incorporate banner ads, interstitial ads, or rewarded video ads.

5. In-App Purchases (IAPs)

- **Definition:** IAPs allow users to buy virtual goods, premium content, or services within your app. This model complements freemium apps.

- **Benefits:** IAPs can drive revenue while keeping your app free to download.

- **Examples:** Games often sell in-game currency, items, or upgrades via IAPs.

6. Sponsorships and Partnerships

- **Definition:** Partner with other companies or brands for sponsorships or partnerships within your app. This can include sponsored content or features.

- **Benefits:** Sponsorships can provide a significant source of revenue, especially if your app has a large and engaged user base.

- **Examples:** Social media apps may partner with brands for sponsored posts or features.

7. Donations

- **Definition:** Allow users to make voluntary donations to support your app. This approach relies on the goodwill of your user community.

- **Benefits:** While not a primary revenue source, donations can provide some financial support.

- **Examples:** Apps or software developed by independent creators may include a "Donate" option.

8. Affiliate Marketing

- **Definition:** Promote products or services from other companies within your app and earn commissions on sales generated through your referrals.

- **Benefits:** This model can work well for apps that cater to specific niches or industries.

- **Examples:** Content apps may include affiliate links to products or services they recommend.

9. Data Monetization

- **Definition:** If your app collects user data, you can anonymize and aggregate this data and sell insights to third parties.

- **Benefits:** Data monetization can be a supplementary revenue stream, but it requires careful handling of user data and privacy.

- **Examples:** Some fitness apps share anonymized data with healthcare researchers.

10. E-commerce Integration

- **Definition:** If your app fits an e-commerce niche, consider integrating e-commerce functionality and earning a commission on sales.

- **Benefits:** This model is suitable for apps that can facilitate transactions, such as shopping or travel apps.

- **Examples:** Retail apps often allow users to browse and purchase products.

Choosing the right monetization strategy depends on your app's nature, target audience, and goals. You may also opt for a combination of these strategies to maximize revenue. It's essential to strike a balance between monetization and providing value to your users to ensure the long-term success of your iOS app.

Section 17.2: Implementing In-App Purchases

Implementing in-app purchases (IAPs) is a common way to monetize your iOS app, especially if you're following the freemium model. IAPs allow users to buy virtual goods, premium content, or services within your app. This section will guide you through the process of adding IAPs to your iOS app.

1. Set Up Your App in App Store Connect

Before implementing IAPs, you need to configure your app in App Store Connect[1]. Here's what you need to do:

- Create an App Store Connect record for your app if you haven't already.

- Enable In-App Purchases in your app's App Store Connect settings.

1. https://appstoreconnect.apple.com/

2. Create IAP Products

In the App Store Connect dashboard, navigate to "My Apps" and select your app. Then, go to the "Features" tab and choose "In-App Purchases." Here, you can create different IAP products, such as consumables, non-consumables, subscriptions, and more.

For each product, you'll need to specify details like the product ID, pricing, and availability. Apple provides guidelines on how to set up these products correctly.

3. Integrate StoreKit Framework

In your Xcode project, you'll need to integrate the StoreKit framework to handle IAP transactions. To do this:

- Import the StoreKit framework into your project.
- Create an SKProductsRequest to fetch product information from the App Store.
- Implement delegate methods to handle the response from the product request.

```
import StoreKit

// Request product information

let productIdentifiers: Set<String> = ["com.yourapp.productID"]

let productsRequest = SKProductsRequest(productIdentifiers: productIdentifiers)

productsRequest.delegate = self

productsRequest.start()
```

4. Handle IAP Transactions

Once you have retrieved product information, you can allow users to make purchases. Implement the following steps:

- Display the products to the user.
- When a user selects a product to purchase, initiate the transaction using SKPaymentQueue.

```
if let product = availableProducts.first {
let payment = SKPayment(product: product)
SKPaymentQueue.default().add(payment)
}
```

- Implement the SKPaymentTransactionObserver protocol to handle transaction updates. You'll receive callbacks when transactions are initiated, completed, or failed.

5. Unlock Purchased Content

After a successful purchase, you'll need to unlock or deliver the purchased content to the user. Typically, this involves updating the app's UI or enabling access to premium features.

6. Restore Purchases

Apple requires that you provide a way for users to restore their purchases. Implement a "Restore Purchases" button or option that calls SKPaymentQueue.default().restoreCompletedTransactions() to restore any previous purchases.

7. Test IAPs

Before submitting your app to the App Store, thoroughly test your IAPs in a sandbox environment. Apple provides sandbox user accounts for testing, allowing you to verify that your purchase flow works correctly.

8. Handle Receipt Validation

To prevent fraudulent purchases, it's essential to validate purchase receipts with Apple's servers. This ensures that the purchase was made legitimately.

9. Comply with Apple's Guidelines

Be sure to read and adhere to Apple's guidelines[2] regarding IAPs, especially concerning pricing, user consent, and content offerings.

Implementing in-app purchases can be complex, but it's a powerful way to generate revenue for your app. It's essential to follow best practices, provide a seamless user experience, and ensure compliance with Apple's policies to create a successful IAP strategy.

Section 17.3: Managing Subscriptions

Managing subscriptions is a crucial aspect of running an app that offers subscription-based services or content. Subscriptions can provide a steady stream of revenue and keep users engaged with your app over an extended period. In this section, we'll explore how to manage subscriptions effectively in your iOS app.

2. https://developer.apple.com/app-store/review/guidelines/#in-app-purchase

1. Types of Subscriptions

Before diving into subscription management, it's essential to understand the types of subscriptions your app offers. iOS supports various subscription models, including:

- **Auto-Renewable Subscriptions:** These renew automatically unless the user cancels them. Common for services like streaming platforms.
- **Non-Renewing Subscriptions:** These don't renew automatically and require users to purchase them again manually. Useful for fixed-duration content access.

2. Implementing Subscriptions

To implement subscriptions in your app, you'll need to:

- Create and configure your subscription products in App Store Connect.
- Use the StoreKit framework to handle subscription transactions, similar to in-app purchases (IAPs). This includes displaying subscription options, initiating purchases, and handling transactions.

```
import StoreKit

// Display subscription options

let productIdentifiers: Set<String> = ["com.yourapp.subscription"]

let productsRequest = SKProductsRequest(productIdentifiers: productIdentifiers)

productsRequest.delegate = self
```

```
productsRequest.start()

// Initiating a subscription purchase

if let product = availableProducts.first {

let payment = SKPayment(product: product)

SKPaymentQueue.default().add(payment)

}
```

- Implement a user interface for managing subscriptions, allowing users to subscribe, view subscription details, and cancel subscriptions.

3. Subscription States

Managing subscription states is vital for ensuring that users have access to the content or services they've subscribed to. You should monitor and handle the following states:

- **Active:** The user's subscription is active, and they should have full access to the subscribed content or services.

- **Expired:** The subscription has expired, and the user's access to premium content or services should be restricted.

- **Grace Period:** Apple provides a grace period during which users can renew their subscription without losing access.

4. Receipt Validation

To verify the authenticity of a user's subscription, perform receipt validation with Apple's servers. This ensures that the user's subscription is legitimate and hasn't been tampered with.

5. Subscription Management UI

Create a user-friendly interface for managing subscriptions within your app. This should allow users to:

- **Subscribe:** Provide a clear and straightforward way for users to initiate a subscription.

- **View Subscription Details:** Show users their current subscription details, including the renewal date and price.

- **Cancel Subscription:** Implement a way for users to cancel their subscription within the app.

6. Handling Grace Periods and Renewals

During grace periods, users can renew their subscriptions without losing access to content. Implement logic to handle these scenarios and notify users when their subscription is about to expire.

7. Consideration for Users' Data

Respect users' data and privacy. Ensure that your subscription management system complies with data protection regulations, such as GDPR.

8. Testing Subscriptions

Before launching your app, thoroughly test subscription flows in a sandbox environment using test accounts provided by Apple.

9. Communicate Changes

If you plan to change subscription prices or terms, communicate these changes clearly to existing subscribers and follow Apple's guidelines regarding pricing changes.

Effective subscription management can help you maintain a loyal user base and generate recurring revenue for your app. It's essential to strike a balance between offering value to subscribers and adhering to best practices and regulations. By providing a seamless and transparent subscription experience, you can build trust with your users and encourage long-term subscriptions.

Section 17.4: Handling Payments and Receipts

Handling payments and receipts is a critical aspect of running an iOS app that offers subscription-based services or in-app purchases. It involves managing transactions, keeping records of purchases, and ensuring the integrity of the payment process. In this section, we'll explore how to effectively handle payments and receipts in your iOS app.

1. Transaction Processing

When a user makes a purchase or subscription, it generates a transaction. It's essential to process these transactions correctly and promptly. You can use the StoreKit framework to handle transactions. Here's a basic example:

```
import StoreKit

// Implement the SKPaymentTransactionObserver protocol
```

```
class PaymentTransactionObserver: NSObject, SKPaymentTransactionObserver {

func paymentQueue(_ queue: SKPaymentQueue, updatedTransactions transactions: [SKPaymentTransaction]) {

for transaction in transactions {

switch transaction.transactionState {

case .purchased:

// Handle a successful purchase

// Provide the purchased content or services to the user

SKPaymentQueue.default().finishTransaction(transaction)

case .failed:

// Handle a failed purchase

// Inform the user and possibly offer a retry option

SKPaymentQueue.default().finishTransaction(transaction)

case .restored:

// Handle a restored purchase (e.g., for non-renewing subscriptions)

// Provide the restored content or services to the user

SKPaymentQueue.default().finishTransaction(transaction)

default:

break

}
```

```
}
}
}
```

2. Receipt Validation

Receipt validation is crucial to ensure that the user's purchase or subscription is legitimate and hasn't been tampered with. You should regularly validate receipts with Apple's servers, typically in a secure server environment. Here's a simplified example of receipt validation in Swift:

```
func validateReceipt() {
guard let appStoreReceiptURL = Bundle.main.appStoreReceiptURL,
FileManager.default.fileExists(atPath: appStoreReceiptURL.path) else {
// No receipt found; handle this case
return
}
do {
let receiptData = try Data(contentsOf: appStoreReceiptURL)
let receiptString = receiptData.base64EncodedString(options: [])
// Send the receiptString to your server for validation
} catch {
```

```
// Handle the error
}
}
```

3. Record Keeping

Maintain a record of all transactions and receipts associated with your app. This record should include details like transaction IDs, purchase dates, and product information. Proper record-keeping is essential for customer support, dispute resolution, and compliance.

4. Handling Refunds and Disputes

Occasionally, users may request refunds or dispute charges. Apple provides a resolution center in App Store Connect for handling these cases. Be prepared to respond to refund requests promptly and follow Apple's guidelines.

5. Testing Transactions

Before releasing your app, thoroughly test transaction flows, including purchases and subscriptions, in a sandbox environment using test accounts provided by Apple. Ensure that both successful and failed transactions are handled gracefully.

6. Payment Processing Security

Security is paramount when dealing with payments. Ensure that your app complies with security best practices and standards. Use secure connections (HTTPS) for transmitting payment information and protect sensitive user data.

7. Localization of Pricing and Payment Methods

Consider localizing your app's pricing and payment methods to make users from different regions feel comfortable when making purchases. Offer multiple payment options if possible to cater to a broader audience.

8. Communicating Payment Policies

Clearly communicate your app's payment policies, including pricing, billing frequency, and refund policies, to users before they make purchases or subscribe. Transparency can help prevent disputes.

Handling payments and receipts effectively not only ensures a smooth user experience but also maintains the integrity of your app's revenue stream. By implementing secure and reliable payment processing, you can build trust with your users and provide a hassle-free purchasing experience.

Section 17.5: Maximizing Revenue from Your App

Generating revenue from your iOS app is a crucial aspect of app development, especially if you're running a business or offering premium services. Maximizing revenue involves various strategies and considerations that go beyond just creating a great app. In this section, we'll explore strategies and best practices to help you make the most of your app's revenue potential.

1. Diversify Monetization Models

Consider using multiple monetization models to reach a broader audience. Common models include:

• **Freemium**: Offer a free version of your app with limited features and a premium version with additional features or content for a fee.

• **In-App Purchases**: Sell digital goods, services, or content within your app, such as virtual items or subscriptions.

• **Ads**: Implement in-app advertising through networks like Google AdMob or Facebook Audience Network.

• **Subscriptions**: Offer subscription plans with recurring revenue. Ensure your app provides ongoing value to subscribers.

• **Affiliate Marketing**: Promote products or services from other companies and earn a commission for each sale generated through your app.

2. Optimize Pricing Strategies

Pricing is a critical factor in revenue generation. Consider these pricing strategies:

• **A/B Testing**: Experiment with different price points to find the optimal one that maximizes revenue without deterring users.

• **Segmented Pricing**: Offer tiered pricing options to cater to different user segments. Some users may prefer lower-cost options, while others may value premium features.

- **Discounts and Promotions**: Periodically offer discounts or promotions to attract new users and encourage purchases.

3. Leverage Analytics

Use analytics tools to gain insights into user behavior and revenue sources. Monitor key metrics such as user retention, conversion rates, and lifetime value. Data-driven decisions can lead to more effective monetization strategies.

4. Customer Support and Engagement

Provide excellent customer support to address user concerns and issues promptly. Engage with your users through feedback channels and social media. Happy users are more likely to make purchases and recommend your app to others.

5. App Store Optimization (ASO)

Optimize your app's visibility on the App Store by using relevant keywords, compelling descriptions, and eye-catching visuals. Higher visibility can lead to more downloads and potential revenue.

6. Localize Your App

Consider localizing your app for different regions and languages. This can expand your user base and increase revenue from international markets.

7. User Feedback and Iteration

Regularly collect user feedback and use it to improve your app. Iteration based on user input can lead to a better user experience and, consequently, higher revenue.

8. Performance Optimization

Ensure that your app performs well and is free of major bugs. Users are more likely to make purchases in a stable and responsive app.

9. Data Privacy and Compliance

Adhere to data privacy regulations and best practices, such as GDPR or CCPA, to build trust with users and avoid legal issues.

10. Explore Partnerships

Consider partnerships with other apps or businesses that align with your target audience. Cross-promotion or co-marketing can help you reach a wider user base.

11. Regularly Update Your App

Keep your app fresh by releasing regular updates with new features, bug fixes, and optimizations. This keeps users engaged and may lead to increased revenue.

12. Stay Informed About Trends

Keep an eye on industry trends and emerging technologies. Being early to adopt new technologies or trends can give your app a competitive edge.

Maximizing revenue from your iOS app is an ongoing process that requires a combination of smart monetization strategies, user engagement, and continuous improvement. By implementing these strategies and staying attentive to your users' needs, you can build a sustainable source of revenue from your app.

Chapter 18: Accessibility and Inclusivity

Accessibility and inclusivity are fundamental principles in modern app development. Ensuring that your iOS app can be used by individuals with disabilities is both ethically responsible and beneficial for your app's reach. In this chapter, we will delve into accessibility practices and how to create apps that are inclusive and usable by a diverse audience.

Section 18.1: Designing Accessible Interfaces

What Is Accessibility?

Accessibility, often abbreviated as "a11y," refers to the practice of designing products, services, or environments to be usable by as many people as possible, including those with disabilities. In the context of iOS app development, accessibility means making your app functional and understandable to users with disabilities, such as visual or hearing impairments.

Why Is Accessibility Important?

Accessibility is not just about compliance with legal standards; it's about ensuring that everyone, regardless of their abilities, can access and use your app. Here are some key reasons why accessibility is important:

1. **Inclusivity**: Accessibility extends your app's reach to a broader and more diverse audience, including people with disabilities.
2. **Legal Requirements**: Many countries have laws and regulations that mandate accessibility compliance. Non-compliance can lead to legal issues and fines.

3. **Improved User Experience**: Accessibility features often enhance the overall user experience, even for users without disabilities. For example, voice commands can be useful for hands-free operation.
4. **Positive Brand Image**: Demonstrating a commitment to accessibility can improve your brand's image and reputation.

Designing Accessible Interfaces

To create accessible interfaces, consider the following best practices:

1. Semantic HTML

Use semantic HTML elements to provide meaning to the content. For example, use headings (<h1>, <h2>, etc.), lists (<ul>, <ol>), and labels (<label>) appropriately. Screen readers rely on these elements to convey information to users.

2. Keyboard Accessibility

Ensure that all interactive elements, such as buttons and form fields, can be navigated and activated using only a keyboard. Avoid relying on mouse-specific actions like hover.

3. Alt Text for Images

Include descriptive alternative text (alt text) for images. This helps users with visual impairments understand the content of images. For decorative images, use empty alt text (alt="") to indicate they are purely decorative.

4. High Contrast and Readable Fonts

Choose color combinations with sufficient contrast to make text and UI elements legible. Use clear and readable fonts. Avoid using color as the sole means of conveying information.

5. VoiceOver Support

Test your app with VoiceOver, iOS's built-in screen reader. Ensure that all content and interactive elements are properly labeled and navigable using VoiceOver gestures.

6. Dynamic Type

Support Dynamic Type by using system font styles and allowing users to adjust text size in their device settings. This benefits users with varying levels of visual acuity.

7. Closed Captions and Subtitles

Include closed captions and subtitles for multimedia content, especially for videos with spoken content. This benefits users with hearing impairments.

8. ARIA Roles and Attributes

Use ARIA (Accessible Rich Internet Applications) roles and attributes to enhance the accessibility of web content within your app. ARIA can help convey complex interactions and relationships to screen readers.

9. Testing with Accessibility Tools

Regularly test your app's accessibility using built-in tools like the Accessibility Inspector in Xcode. Additionally, involve users with disabilities in usability testing to gather valuable feedback.

10. Stay Informed

Accessibility guidelines and best practices evolve. Stay informed about the latest standards and recommendations, such as the Web Content Accessibility Guidelines (WCAG) for web content.

By following these accessibility principles and best practices, you can create iOS apps that are inclusive, user-friendly, and compliant with accessibility standards. This not only benefits users with disabilities but also enhances your app's reputation and user base. In the following sections, we'll explore more aspects of accessibility and inclusivity in iOS development.

Section 18.2: VoiceOver and Assistive Technologies

VoiceOver is a powerful assistive technology built into iOS devices that provides spoken feedback to users with visual impairments. It reads aloud the contents of the screen and allows users to navigate and interact with apps using touch gestures and voice commands. Understanding how VoiceOver works and how to make your app compatible with it is crucial for creating accessible iOS applications.

How VoiceOver Works

VoiceOver uses a combination of spoken language and touch gestures to help users navigate and interact with iOS apps. Some fundamental aspects of VoiceOver include:

1. **Speech Output**: VoiceOver reads the elements on the screen, such as text, buttons, and labels, to the user in a synthesized voice.
2. **Gesture Navigation**: Users with visual impairments can navigate through the app's interface using touch gestures that trigger VoiceOver commands. For example, swiping left or right moves between elements, and double-tapping activates an element.
3. **Custom Gestures**: VoiceOver users can define custom gestures to perform specific actions within an app.
4. **Rotor Control**: The VoiceOver Rotor is a virtual dial that allows users to adjust various settings, such as changing the speech rate, navigating by headings or links, and more.

Designing for VoiceOver Compatibility

To ensure your app is VoiceOver-compatible, consider the following guidelines:

1. Accessibility Labels and Traits

Every interactive element in your app, such as buttons, labels, and form fields, should have meaningful accessibility labels and traits. Accessibility labels provide VoiceOver with a description of the element, while traits convey its purpose or behavior. For example, a "Submit" button should have an accessibility label of "Submit" and a trait of "Button."

submitButton.accessibilityLabel = "Submit"

submitButton.accessibilityTraits = .button

2. Organized Content

Organize your app's content logically so that VoiceOver users can navigate it easily. Use headings, lists, and tables when appropriate to create a clear and structured hierarchy.

3. Custom Gestures

If your app has custom gestures or interactions, ensure that VoiceOver users can access and understand them. Provide clear instructions within your app's accessibility documentation or settings.

4. Testing with VoiceOver

Regularly test your app with VoiceOver enabled to identify and address accessibility issues. Use VoiceOver gestures to interact with your app and verify that all elements are properly labeled and navigable.

5. Dynamic Content

If your app displays dynamic content, such as updates or notifications, VoiceOver should announce these changes to the user. You can use the UIAccessibility.post(notification:object:) method to notify VoiceOver of content updates.

UIAccessibility.post(notification: .announcement, argument: "New message received")

6. VoiceOver Rotor

Ensure that VoiceOver users can effectively use the Rotor to adjust settings and navigate your app. Implement the necessary accessibility traits and actions for elements like headings, links, and buttons.

7. Accessibility Inspector

Xcode provides an Accessibility Inspector tool that allows you to examine your app's accessibility properties and test VoiceOver interactions. Use this tool to identify and resolve accessibility issues during development.

Additional Assistive Technologies

In addition to VoiceOver, iOS devices offer various other assistive technologies, including:

- **Switch Control**: Allows users to control their device using external adaptive switches.
- **Magnifier**: Provides a digital magnification of the screen for users with visual impairments.
- **Speak Selection**: Reads selected text aloud to the user.
- **Guided Access**: Limits the device to a single app and restricts touch input to specific areas of the screen.

By designing your app to be compatible with these technologies, you can ensure that it's accessible to a wide range of users with different needs. Accessibility isn't just a checkbox; it's a commitment to making your app usable and inclusive for everyone.

Section 18.3: Testing for Accessibility

Accessibility is a critical aspect of iOS app development, as it ensures that your app is usable by a wide range of individuals, including those with disabilities. To ensure that your app is accessible, it's essential to perform thorough accessibility testing. In this section, we'll explore the importance of accessibility testing, tools available for testing, and best practices to follow.

The Importance of Accessibility Testing

Accessibility testing helps identify and address issues that may prevent users with disabilities from using your app effectively. It ensures that your app provides an inclusive experience, meeting legal requirements and improving your app's reputation. Failing to address accessibility issues can result in user frustration, legal consequences, and a smaller user base.

Accessibility Testing Tools

iOS provides various tools and features to assist with accessibility testing:

1. Accessibility Inspector: Xcode includes an Accessibility Inspector tool that allows you to inspect the accessibility properties of UI elements in your app. You can use this tool to verify that elements have appropriate labels, traits, and other attributes.

2. VoiceOver: VoiceOver, an assistive technology built into iOS, provides spoken feedback to users with visual impairments. Enabling VoiceOver during testing allows you to experience your app as a visually impaired user would.

3. Accessibility Settings: iOS has accessibility settings that let you simulate different scenarios, such as grayscale mode, reduced transparency, and color filters. These settings help you understand how users with specific visual needs perceive your app.

4. Screen Curtain: Screen Curtain is an accessibility feature that turns off the display while keeping the touch screen active. It helps you test your app's compatibility with VoiceOver without relying on visual feedback.

Best Practices for Accessibility Testing

When conducting accessibility testing for your iOS app, consider the following best practices:

1. Regular Testing: Integrate accessibility testing into your development process, not just as a final step. Test early and often to catch issues as they arise.

2. Use Real Devices: Test on real iOS devices, as their behavior may differ from simulators or desktop testing tools.

3. Test with VoiceOver: Enable VoiceOver on a device and use it to navigate and interact with your app. Pay attention to how elements are read aloud and if the order of navigation makes sense.

4. Test Different Scenarios: Use accessibility settings to simulate various scenarios, such as increased text size, bold text, and different color filters. Ensure that your app remains usable under these conditions.

5. Manual and Automated Testing: Perform manual testing, but also consider using automated testing tools and frameworks designed for accessibility testing. They can help identify common issues more efficiently.

6. Accessibility Testing Checklist: Create a checklist of accessibility features and elements to test for, such as labels, traits, focus order, and color contrast. Refer to this checklist during testing to ensure thorough coverage.

7. Collaborate with Accessibility Experts: If possible, involve individuals with disabilities or accessibility experts in your testing process. Their feedback can be invaluable in identifying issues and suggesting improvements.

8. Update Accessibility Documentation: Ensure that your app's accessibility documentation is up to date and accurate. This documentation should provide users with guidance on how to use accessibility features in your app.

9. Regression Testing: After making accessibility improvements, perform regression testing to verify that existing features remain accessible.

10. Stay Informed: Stay updated on the latest accessibility guidelines and best practices from organizations like the Web Content Accessibility Guidelines (WCAG) and Apple's Accessibility Guidelines.

By following these best practices and dedicating time to accessibility testing, you can create iOS apps that are not only functional but also accessible to all users, regardless of their abilities. Making accessibility a priority is a commitment to inclusivity and a better user experience for everyone.

Section 18.4: Legal Requirements and Compliance

Ensuring that your iOS app is legally compliant is a crucial aspect of app development. Failing to meet legal requirements can lead to serious consequences, including lawsuits and removal from app stores. In this section, we'll explore the legal considerations you should be aware of when developing iOS apps.

Privacy and Data Protection

1. General Data Protection Regulation (GDPR): If your app collects personal data from users in the European Union, you must comply with GDPR regulations. This includes obtaining explicit consent for data collection, providing data access and deletion options, and ensuring data security.

2. Children's Online Privacy Protection Act (COPPA): If your app is targeted at children under the age of 13 in the United States, you must comply with COPPA. This involves obtaining parental consent for data collection and adhering to strict privacy practices.

3. California Consumer Privacy Act (CCPA): If your app collects personal information from California residents, CCPA regulations apply. This includes providing users with the right to know what data is collected and the ability to opt-out of data sales.

Intellectual Property

4. Copyright: Ensure that you have the legal rights to use any images, music, or other content in your app. Unauthorized use of copyrighted material can lead to legal action.

5. Trademarks: Avoid using trademarks owned by other companies in your app's name, logo, or content. Trademark infringement can result in legal disputes.

Accessibility

6. Accessibility Laws: In various regions, there are laws and regulations that require digital content, including mobile apps, to be accessible to individuals with disabilities. Compliance often involves meeting specific accessibility standards, such as WCAG.

Terms of Service and Privacy Policy

7. Terms of Service (ToS): Clearly outline the terms and conditions that users must agree to when using your app. Specify user responsibilities, limitations of liability, and dispute resolution mechanisms.

8. Privacy Policy: Inform users about what data you collect, how it's used, and who it's shared with. Your privacy policy should be easily accessible within the app.

Security

9. Data Security: Protect user data from breaches by implementing strong security measures, such as encryption and secure storage.

10. App Store Guidelines: Comply with the guidelines set by app stores, such as Apple's App Store Review Guidelines. Failure to do so can result in app removal.

Accessibility Compliance

11. Accessibility Features: Ensure your app includes accessibility features to make it usable by individuals with disabilities. This includes features like VoiceOver support, resizable text, and alternative text for images.

Consult with Legal Experts

12. Legal Counsel: Consider consulting with legal experts who specialize in technology and app development to ensure compliance with all relevant laws and regulations.

13. Regular Updates: Stay informed about changes in laws and regulations related to app development. Regularly update your app and its legal documentation to remain compliant.

Remember that legal compliance is an ongoing process, and it's essential to make it a priority from the early stages of development. Failure to comply with legal requirements can not only harm your app's reputation but also result in severe financial and legal consequences. Therefore, it's crucial to stay informed, seek legal advice when needed, and prioritize the protection of user data and intellectual property.

Section 18.5: Creating Inclusive iOS Apps

Inclusivity is a fundamental principle of iOS app development. Creating apps that are accessible to a wide range of users, including those with disabilities, not only broadens your app's audience but also adheres to ethical and legal standards. In this section, we'll explore strategies for creating inclusive iOS apps.

1. Understanding Accessibility Guidelines

To create an inclusive app, it's crucial to understand the accessibility guidelines provided by Apple, including the Web Content Accessibility Guidelines (WCAG) and the Human Interface Guidelines (HIG). These guidelines offer valuable insights into designing and developing apps that cater to diverse user needs.

2. Use Adaptive Layouts

Implementing adaptive layouts allows your app's user interface to adjust to various screen sizes and orientations. Utilize Auto Layout and size classes to ensure your app looks and functions well on different iOS devices.

3. VoiceOver Support

VoiceOver is a screen-reading feature on iOS devices that assists users with visual impairments. Ensure that your app provides meaningful descriptions for interface elements, buttons, and images. Test your app with VoiceOver to verify that it's navigable and understandable using auditory feedback.

4. Dynamic Text and Font Adjustment

Allow users to adjust text size in your app to accommodate their preferences. This feature is especially important for users with visual impairments. Use dynamic type and scalable fonts to ensure that text remains readable at different sizes.

5. High Contrast and Dark Mode

Offer high-contrast themes and support iOS's Dark Mode. These options can improve usability for users with low vision or those who prefer different color schemes.

6. Alternative Text for Images

Include alternative text (alt text) for images, providing concise descriptions of visual content. This helps users with visual impairments understand the context of images.

7. Keyboard Navigation

Make sure that all interactive elements in your app are navigable and usable through keyboard input. Keyboard navigation is essential for users who cannot use touch gestures or a mouse.

8. Testing with Assistive Technologies

Regularly test your app with assistive technologies like VoiceOver and Switch Control. Familiarize yourself with these tools to identify and resolve accessibility issues effectively.

9. Accessible Multimedia

Ensure that videos and audio content in your app are accessible. Provide captions and transcripts for videos and include controls for adjusting audio volume and playback speed.

10. Avoid Exclusive Gestures

Avoid relying solely on complex or multi-finger gestures, as they can be challenging for some users. Whenever possible, provide alternative methods for performing actions.

11. Support for Switch Control

Switch Control is an accessibility feature that enables users to control their devices with external switches. Ensure that your app is compatible with these input methods.

12. Inclusive Design Thinking

From the initial design phase, involve a diverse group of users, including those with disabilities, to provide feedback and insights.

This approach, known as inclusive design thinking, can lead to more inclusive and user-friendly app experiences.

13. Accessibility Labeling for Custom UI Elements

If you create custom UI elements, ensure they have proper accessibility labeling and traits. This makes them usable with VoiceOver and other assistive technologies.

14. Accessibility Audits

Conduct regular accessibility audits of your app, both manually and with automated tools. Address issues promptly to maintain a high level of inclusivity.

15. User Education

Consider providing in-app guidance on accessibility features. Educate users about how to enable and use accessibility features specific to your app.

By prioritizing inclusivity in your iOS app development process, you not only contribute to a more accessible digital environment but also potentially increase your app's user base. Inclusivity is not just a moral imperative but also a valuable design principle that benefits everyone.

Chapter 19: Advanced Topics in iOS Development

In this chapter, we delve into advanced topics in iOS development that can take your skills to the next level. These topics are more specialized and can open up new possibilities for your iOS apps.

Section 19.1: Core Animation and Graphics

Core Animation is a powerful framework in iOS that allows you to create stunning animations and visual effects. It's not just for games; you can use Core Animation to enhance the user interface of your apps and provide a more engaging experience.

1. Understanding Core Animation

Core Animation is the framework responsible for animating views and graphics in iOS. It operates at a low level, allowing for smooth animations and transitions. It's based on a graphics rendering model that is GPU-accelerated, ensuring high performance.

2. Layer-Based Animation

In Core Animation, everything is about layers. CALayer objects represent the visual content of your app. You can animate properties of these layers, such as position, size, opacity, and more, to create visually appealing effects.

3. Implicit and Explicit Animations

Core Animation supports two types of animations: implicit and explicit. Implicit animations are built into certain properties and animate automatically when you change their values. Explicit animations are custom animations that you define and control.

4. Keyframe Animations

Keyframe animations allow you to specify a series of values or "keyframes" for a property over time. This gives you precise control over complex animations.

5. Transformations and 3D Effects

Core Animation supports 2D and 3D transformations, enabling you to rotate, scale, and translate layers in three-dimensional space. This is useful for creating immersive user interfaces and games.

6. Layer Masking and Blending

You can use layer masking to create complex visual effects by revealing or hiding parts of a layer based on a mask layer's shape. Layer blending allows you to combine layers in various ways to create unique visuals.

7. Advanced Animation Timing

Core Animation provides advanced timing functions that let you control the pacing of your animations. You can create ease-in, ease-out, bounce, and custom timing curves.

8. Performance Optimization

Optimizing the performance of your Core Animation animations is crucial for a smooth user experience. Techniques such as rasterization, grouping animations, and reusing layers can help improve performance.

9. Drawing with Core Graphics

Core Animation can also be used for custom drawing using Core Graphics. You can draw shapes, images, and text directly onto a layer, allowing for custom visual elements.

10. Practical Use Cases

We'll explore practical use cases for Core Animation, such as creating animated transitions, interactive gestures, and attention-grabbing visual effects.

As you delve into Core Animation and graphics, you'll discover the immense potential for enhancing the user experience of your iOS apps. Whether you're building games, interactive interfaces, or simply want to add some visual flair to your app, Core Animation is a valuable tool in your arsenal.

Section 19.2: Core Bluetooth and IoT Integration

In this section, we'll explore Core Bluetooth, a framework that enables your iOS apps to communicate with nearby Bluetooth devices. This is particularly valuable for integrating your app with the Internet of Things (IoT) and other Bluetooth-enabled hardware.

1. Introduction to Core Bluetooth

Core Bluetooth is a framework that allows your iOS device to discover, connect to, and communicate with nearby Bluetooth devices, including peripherals like heart rate monitors, fitness trackers, smartwatches, and IoT devices.

2. Bluetooth Low Energy (BLE)

Core Bluetooth primarily focuses on Bluetooth Low Energy (BLE) devices, which are energy-efficient and well-suited for IoT applications. BLE devices consume minimal power, making them ideal for battery-operated devices.

3. Scanning for Peripherals

Your iOS app can scan for nearby BLE peripherals using Core Bluetooth. When you find a peripheral you want to interact with, you can establish a connection to it.

4. Peripheral Services and Characteristics

BLE peripherals expose services that contain characteristics with data you can read from or write to. Understanding the services and characteristics provided by a peripheral is essential for effective communication.

5. Central and Peripheral Roles

In a Core Bluetooth connection, your iOS device can take on either the central role (initiating connections and scanning for peripherals) or the peripheral role (advertising services and characteristics).

6. Background Mode and Beacons

Core Bluetooth works even when your app is in the background, making it suitable for scenarios like beacon technology, where devices broadcast information to nearby smartphones.

7. Handling Bluetooth State

You must handle the Bluetooth state in your app, as users can disable Bluetooth. Core Bluetooth provides notifications to inform your app about changes in Bluetooth availability.

8. Security and Privacy

Security is crucial when communicating with Bluetooth devices. Core Bluetooth includes features for pairing and securing connections, ensuring data privacy and integrity.

9. Real-World Use Cases

We'll explore real-world use cases for Core Bluetooth, such as creating a fitness tracking app that connects to heart rate monitors, controlling IoT devices, or building applications for location-based services.

10. Best Practices and Considerations

We'll discuss best practices for developing iOS apps that integrate with Bluetooth devices, including handling disconnections, managing multiple peripherals, and optimizing power consumption.

11. Bluetooth Beyond iOS

Core Bluetooth is not limited to iOS-to-iOS communication. You can also use it to communicate with non-iOS devices, making it a versatile tool for IoT and cross-platform integration.

Integrating Core Bluetooth into your iOS apps opens up exciting possibilities for connecting to a wide range of Bluetooth-enabled devices and building innovative IoT solutions. Whether you're building a health and fitness app, a home automation solution, or any application that requires wireless communication, Core Bluetooth is a valuable resource for iOS developers.

Section 19.3: Augmented Reality with ARKit

In this section, we will dive into Augmented Reality (AR) development using ARKit, Apple's framework for building immersive AR experiences on iOS devices. ARKit enables developers to blend digital content with the real world, creating interactive and engaging applications.

1. Introduction to ARKit

ARKit is a framework introduced by Apple that allows developers to create augmented reality experiences for iOS devices. It provides a suite of tools and capabilities for detecting surfaces, tracking objects, and rendering 3D content in the real world.

2. ARKit Features

ARKit offers several key features, including:

- **World Tracking:** ARKit can track the device's position and orientation in the real world, allowing digital objects to be placed accurately.

- **Scene Understanding:** It can detect surfaces like tables, floors, and walls, enabling virtual objects to interact with the physical environment.

- **Light Estimation:** ARKit analyzes lighting conditions and adjusts the virtual objects' lighting to match the real world, enhancing realism.

• **Face Tracking:** ARKit supports face tracking for applications involving facial recognition and expression tracking.

3. Creating AR Experiences

To create AR experiences with ARKit, you'll typically follow these steps:

a. **Setting Up the AR Session:** You initialize an AR session to start capturing data from the device's camera and motion sensors.
b. **Detecting Features:** ARKit can detect features like surfaces and objects. You can use these features to anchor virtual objects to the real world.
c. **Rendering 3D Content:** You create or import 3D models and render them in the AR scene, taking into account lighting and positioning.
d. **User Interaction:** ARKit supports user interactions with virtual objects, such as tapping, dragging, or gesturing.
e. **Physics and Realism:** You can add physics simulations to your AR scene to make virtual objects interact with each other and the real world convincingly.

4. Use Cases for ARKit

ARKit is used in various applications, including:

• **Gaming:** Creating interactive games that blend with the real world.

• **Retail:** Visualizing furniture or products in the user's physical space before purchase.

- **Education:** Enhancing learning experiences through interactive AR content.

- **Navigation:** Overlaying directions and information on real-world views.

- **Medical:** Assisting in surgical planning and medical training.

5. Tools for ARKit Development

You'll use Xcode and Swift for ARKit development. Xcode provides a rich AR development environment, including a built-in AR scene viewer.

6. Best Practices and Performance Considerations

Developing AR experiences requires attention to performance and user experience. Optimizing 3D models, handling occlusion, and managing memory are crucial for smooth AR interactions.

ARKit opens up a world of possibilities for creating immersive and interactive applications. Whether you want to build games, educational tools, or practical utilities that enhance the real world with digital content, ARKit provides the tools and capabilities to bring your vision to life on iOS devices.

Section 19.4: Machine Learning and Core ML

Machine learning (ML) has become an integral part of iOS development, allowing apps to perform tasks like image recognition, natural language processing, and predictive analytics. In this section, we'll explore how Core ML, Apple's machine learning framework, empowers developers to integrate ML models into their iOS applications.

1. Introduction to Core ML

Core ML is a framework introduced by Apple that simplifies the integration of machine learning models into iOS, macOS, watchOS, and tvOS apps. It provides a streamlined way to use trained ML models to make predictions, analyze data, and enhance user experiences.

2. Core ML Features

Core ML offers several key features:

- **Ease of Integration:** Core ML models can be seamlessly integrated into your Xcode project, making it accessible to developers, even those without extensive ML expertise.
- **Wide Range of Model Types:** Core ML supports various model types, including neural networks, decision trees, and support vector machines.
- **On-Device Processing:** Core ML performs ML tasks on the user's device, ensuring privacy and reducing the need for constant network connectivity.
- **Optimized Performance:** Models are automatically optimized for the device's hardware, ensuring efficient execution.

3. Using Core ML in Your App

To use Core ML in your app, you'll typically follow these steps:

a. **Choose a Pretrained Model or Train Your Own:** You can either use pretrained ML models available in the Core ML library or train custom models using tools like Create ML.
b. **Conversion to Core ML Format:** If you train a custom model, you'll need to convert it to the Core ML format using the Core ML Tools.
c. **Integrate into Your App:** You import the Core ML model into your Xcode project and write code to use the model for inference or predictions.
d. **Enhance User Experience:** You can use ML models to provide personalized recommendations, detect objects, classify images, or analyze text sentiment, depending on your app's requirements.

4. Use Cases for Core ML

Core ML finds applications in various domains, such as:

- **Image Recognition:** Identify objects, scenes, or text within images.

- **Natural Language Processing:** Perform sentiment analysis, language translation, or chatbot interactions.

- **Healthcare:** Analyze medical data, detect anomalies, or assist in diagnosing diseases.

- **Finance:** Predict stock market trends, analyze customer data for fraud detection, or create personalized financial recommendations.

5. Tools for Core ML Development

Xcode provides tools like Core ML Model Composer and Create ML for creating, training, and converting ML models. You can also leverage popular ML libraries like TensorFlow and PyTorch to build custom models.

6. Performance and Efficiency

Efficiency is crucial when using ML models in mobile apps. You should consider factors like model size, inference speed, and power consumption to ensure a smooth user experience.

Core ML brings the power of machine learning to iOS development, enabling developers to create intelligent and responsive applications. Whether you're building a recommendation engine, a language translation tool, or an image recognition app, Core ML provides the tools and infrastructure needed to harness the capabilities of machine learning on Apple devices.

Section 19.5: Cross-Platform Development with SwiftUI

SwiftUI is Apple's modern declarative framework for building user interfaces across all Apple platforms, including iOS, macOS, watchOS, and tvOS. In this section, we'll explore how SwiftUI enables cross-platform development and simplifies the creation of consistent and adaptive user interfaces.

1. Introduction to SwiftUI

SwiftUI was introduced by Apple in 2019 as a successor to UIKit and AppKit. It allows developers to build user interfaces using a declarative syntax, where you describe the desired UI state, and

SwiftUI automatically updates the interface to match that state. This approach simplifies UI development and reduces the amount of boilerplate code.

2. Cross-Platform Capabilities

One of the standout features of SwiftUI is its ability to create user interfaces that work seamlessly across all Apple platforms. Here's how SwiftUI enables cross-platform development:

- **Unified Codebase:** With SwiftUI, you can maintain a single codebase for your app, making it easier to share code and resources across iOS, macOS, watchOS, and tvOS.

- **Adaptive Design:** SwiftUI provides tools for creating adaptive UIs that automatically adjust to different screen sizes and orientations, ensuring a consistent user experience.

- **Platform-Specific Customization:** While sharing code, you can also apply platform-specific customizations to tailor the UI for each device type.

3. SwiftUI Views and Controls

SwiftUI introduces a wide range of views and controls that are platform-agnostic. These include text views, buttons, navigation views, lists, and more. You can combine and customize these elements to create complex user interfaces.

4. Data Binding and State Management

SwiftUI utilizes data binding and state management to connect UI elements with your app's data and logic. When your app's state changes, SwiftUI automatically updates the UI to reflect those changes, reducing the need for manual UI updates.

5. Navigation and Layout

Navigation in SwiftUI is based on a stack-based model, similar to UIKit's navigation controllers. You can easily implement navigation between different views and hierarchies.

Layout in SwiftUI is driven by the concept of stacks and flexible containers. You can use stacks to arrange views horizontally or vertically, and SwiftUI takes care of adapting the layout for various screen sizes and orientations.

6. Integration with Existing UIKit and AppKit Code

SwiftUI can be integrated with existing UIKit and AppKit code, allowing you to gradually adopt SwiftUI in your projects. This is especially useful when migrating older apps to SwiftUI.

7. Preview and Debugging

Xcode offers live previews of your SwiftUI interfaces, making it easier to design and debug your user interfaces in real time. You can see how your UI looks on different devices and in different states without running the app.

8. Accessibility and Localization

SwiftUI includes built-in support for accessibility and localization, ensuring that your app is inclusive and can be easily localized for different languages and regions.

9. Limitations and Compatibility

While SwiftUI offers many advantages, it may not cover all the features and behaviors provided by UIKit or AppKit. Additionally, SwiftUI is available on iOS 13 and later, macOS 10.15 and later, watchOS 6 and later, and tvOS 13 and later, so you'll need to consider compatibility when using it in your projects.

SwiftUI has revolutionized the way developers create user interfaces for Apple platforms. Its cross-platform capabilities, declarative syntax, and integration with existing code make it a powerful choice for modern app development. Whether you're building an app for iOS, macOS, watchOS, or tvOS, SwiftUI provides the tools you need to create elegant and consistent user experiences.

Chapter 20: Future Trends in iOS Development

Section 20.1: Emerging Technologies in iOS

The world of iOS development is dynamic and ever-evolving. In this section, we'll explore some of the emerging technologies that are shaping the future of iOS development. These technologies have the potential to change the way we build and interact with iOS apps.

1. 5G Connectivity

The rollout of 5G networks is set to revolutionize mobile connectivity. With significantly faster download and upload speeds, lower latency, and improved reliability, 5G will enable new possibilities for iOS apps. Developers can leverage 5G to deliver high-quality multimedia content, real-time AR experiences, and more bandwidth-intensive applications.

```
// Example: Checking for 5G connectivity

if let currentRadioAccessTechnology = CTTelephonyNetworkInfo().currentRadioAccessTechnology {

if currentRadioAccessTechnology == CTRadioAccessTechnologyNR {

print("Connected to 5G network")

}

}
```

2. Augmented Reality (AR)

ARKit, Apple's augmented reality framework, continues to evolve. With advancements in AR technology, developers can create immersive AR experiences that blend the digital and physical worlds. From gaming and navigation to education and retail, AR has the potential to transform various industries.

```
// Example: Placing a virtual object in AR

let virtualObject = SCNNode(geometry: SCNBox(width: 0.1, height: 0.1, length: 0.1, chamferRadius: 0))

virtualObject.position = SCNVector3(0, 0, -0.5)

sceneView.scene.rootNode.addChildNode(virtualObject)
```

3. Machine Learning and AI

Core ML, Apple's machine learning framework, allows developers to integrate machine learning models into their apps. As machine learning becomes more accessible, iOS apps can provide personalized experiences, real-time language translation, image recognition, and more. Advances in on-device machine learning models enhance user privacy and reduce latency.

```
// Example: Using Core ML for image classification

let model = MobileNetV2()

if let prediction = try? model.prediction(image: image) {

print("Predicted class: \(prediction.classLabel)")

}
```

4. Privacy and Security

Apple continues to prioritize user privacy and data security. New privacy-focused features and guidelines for app developers are introduced with each iOS update. Staying compliant with these policies and implementing secure coding practices is essential for app success and user trust.

```
// Example: Requesting user's permission for location access

import CoreLocation

let locationManager = CLLocationManager()

locationManager.requestWhenInUseAuthorization()
```

5. Swift Evolution

Swift, the programming language used for iOS development, is under active development. Swift Evolution proposals introduce new language features, optimizations, and improvements. Keeping up with Swift's evolution ensures that your codebase remains modern and efficient.

```
// Example: Using a Swift Evolution proposal feature (Concurrency)

Task {

let result = await fetchUserData()

print("Fetched user data: \(result)")

}
```

6. Cross-Platform Development with SwiftUI

As mentioned in Chapter 19, SwiftUI enables cross-platform development for iOS, macOS, watchOS, and tvOS. Its continued growth and refinement make it an attractive choice for building apps that run seamlessly across Apple devices.

```
// Example: Creating a cross-platform SwiftUI view

struct ContentView: View {

var body: some View {

Text("Hello, SwiftUI!")

}

}
```

7. Voice and Natural Language Processing

Voice assistants and natural language processing (NLP) are becoming increasingly important. SiriKit allows developers to integrate Siri into their apps, opening up opportunities for voice-controlled interactions. Additionally, NLP can be used to extract insights from text data and improve user experiences.

```
// Example: Integrating Siri with your app

import Intents

class MyIntentHandler: NSObject, MyIntentHandling {

func handle(intent: MyIntent, completion: @escaping (MyIntentResponse) -> Void) {

// Handle the intent and provide a response
```

```
}
}
```

8. Internet of Things (IoT) Integration

With the growth of IoT devices, iOS apps are becoming central hubs for controlling and monitoring smart devices. HomeKit provides a framework for integrating IoT devices into the Apple ecosystem, allowing users to manage their smart homes from their iOS devices.

```
// Example: Controlling a smart light with HomeKit
import HomeKit
let homeManager = HMHomeManager()
if let home = homeManager.primaryHome {
for accessory in home.accessories {
if accessory.name == "Living Room Light" {
accessory.togglePower()
}
}
}
```

9. App Clips

App Clips are lightweight parts of an app that users can quickly access without downloading the full app. They provide a seamless way to engage users and offer specific app functionalities when needed.

```
// Example: Defining an App Clip experience

import UIKit

import AppClip

@main

struct MyAppClip: AppClip {

var body: some Scene {


## ASSISTANT

WindowGroup {

ContentView()

}

}

}
```

The future of iOS development is filled with exciting opportunities. By staying informed about these emerging technologies and trends, iOS developers can create innovative and impactful apps that cater to the evolving needs of users in the Apple ecosystem. Whether it's leveraging 5G connectivity, exploring AR experiences, or integrating machine learning, embracing these advancements is key to building the apps of tomorrow.

Section 20.2: The Evolution of Swift

Swift, Apple's open-source programming language, has come a long way since its introduction in 2014. In this section, we'll explore the evolution of Swift and the key features and improvements introduced in various Swift versions.

1. Swift 1.0 (2014)

Swift was initially introduced as a modern, safe, and fast programming language for iOS and macOS app development. It brought significant improvements over Objective-C, with concise syntax, memory safety, and better performance.

```
// Swift 1.0: Basic syntax

let message = "Hello, Swift!"

println(message)
```

2. Swift 2.0 (2015)

Swift 2.0 introduced several new features, including error handling with try, throw, and catch, making code more robust. It also introduced protocol extensions, making it easier to add functionality to types.

```
// Swift 2.0: Error handling

enum NetworkError: Error {

case noInternet

case serverError

}

func fetchData() throws {

// Fetch data from the network

}
```

3. Swift 3.0 (2016)

Swift 3.0 was a major update aimed at improving code consistency and readability. It introduced API design guidelines and made significant changes to the syntax, including removing the NS prefix from Foundation framework types.

```
// Swift 3.0: API naming and syntax changes

let numbers = [1, 2, 3]

let sum = numbers.reduce(0, +)
```

4. Swift 4.0 (2017)

Swift 4.0 focused on enhancing the language's expressiveness. It introduced Codable, a protocol for encoding and decoding data, which simplified working with JSON. It also added key paths for easy access to properties.

```
// Swift 4.0: Codable for JSON parsing

struct Person: Codable {

var name: String

var age: Int

}
```

5. Swift 4.2 (2018)

Swift 4.2 brought improvements to the Swift Package Manager and introduced custom string interpolation, enabling the creation of custom string representations for types.

```
// Swift 4.2: Custom string interpolation
```

```
struct Point {

var x: Int

var y: Int

}

extension Point: CustomStringConvertible {

var description: String {

return "(\(x), \(y))"

}

}
```

6. Swift 5.0 (2019)

Swift 5.0 was a significant milestone, introducing ABI (Application Binary Interface) stability. This ensured that Swift apps no longer needed to include the Swift runtime libraries, reducing app sizes. It also introduced several language enhancements, including raw string literals and result types.

```
// Swift 5.0: Raw string literals

let json = """

{

"name": "John",

"age": 30

}

"""
```

7. Swift 5.1 (2019)

Swift 5.1 introduced property wrappers, enabling the creation of custom property behaviors. It also improved the performance of the Dictionary type and introduced a new diffable data source for table and collection views.

```
// Swift 5.1: Property wrappers

@propertyWrapper

struct Clamped<Value: Comparable> {

private var value: Value

var wrappedValue: Value {

get { return value }

set { value = min(max(newValue, lowerBound), upperBound) }

}

init(wrappedValue: Value, _ range: ClosedRange<Value>) {

lowerBound = range.lowerBound

upperBound = range.upperBound

value = min(max(wrappedValue, lowerBound), upperBound)

}

let lowerBound: Value

let upperBound: Value

}
```

8. Swift 5.5 (2021)

Swift 5.5 introduced concurrency support, which simplifies asynchronous programming. The async and await keywords enable developers to write more readable and maintainable asynchronous code. It also introduced structured concurrency and actors for safer concurrent code.

```
// Swift 5.5: Concurrency with async/await

func fetchUserData() async throws -> UserData {

// Asynchronously fetch user data

}
```

Swift continues to evolve, with new features and improvements introduced in each version. As an iOS developer, staying up-to-date with the latest Swift advancements is crucial to writing efficient, safe, and maintainable code for your iOS apps. The evolution of Swift has made it a powerful and versatile language, and it remains at the forefront of iOS development.

Section 20.3: Trends in User Experience Design

User experience (UX) design plays a pivotal role in the success of iOS apps. As technology evolves, so do user expectations and design trends. In this section, we'll explore some prominent trends in user experience design for iOS apps.

1. Minimalism and Clean Interfaces

Minimalistic design continues to be a popular trend in iOS app development. Clean interfaces with a focus on essential content and intuitive navigation enhance the user experience. Minimalism reduces clutter, making apps more user-friendly.

```
// Minimalistic UI design

let welcomeLabel = UILabel()

welcomeLabel.text = "Welcome to our app"

welcomeLabel.font = UIFont.systemFont(ofSize: 24)

welcomeLabel.textAlignment = .center
```

2. Dark Mode and Light Mode

With the introduction of iOS 13, Apple introduced system-wide Dark Mode. Apps that support both Dark and Light Modes provide users with options to choose their preferred interface style. Designing for both modes ensures accessibility and caters to diverse user preferences.

```
// Supporting Dark Mode

override func traitCollectionDidChange(_ previousTraitCollection: UITraitCollection?) {

super.traitCollectionDidChange(previousTraitCollection)

if self.traitCollection.hasDifferentColorAppearance(comparedTo: previousTraitCollection) {

// Update UI for Dark/Light Mode

}

}
```

3. Microinteractions

Microinteractions are subtle animations or visual cues that provide feedback to users. They can include button animations, loading indicators, or interactive elements. Well-designed microinteractions enhance the overall user experience.

```
// Button animation on tap

UIView.animate(withDuration: 0.2, animations: {

button.transform = CGAffineTransform(scaleX: 0.9, y: 0.9)

}) { _ in

UIView.animate(withDuration: 0.2) {

button.transform = .identity

}

}
```

4. Gesture-Based Navigation

Gesture-based navigation is becoming more prevalent, especially on devices with edge-to-edge displays. Users can swipe, pinch, or tap gestures to navigate within apps. Implementing intuitive gesture controls can make your app feel more modern and responsive.

```
// Gesture recognizer for swipe navigation

let swipeRight = UISwipeGestureRecognizer(target: self, action: #selector(handleSwipe))

swipeRight.direction = .right

view.addGestureRecognizer(swipeRight)
```

5. Personalization and AI

Personalized experiences powered by artificial intelligence (AI) and machine learning (ML) are gaining traction. Apps can recommend content, tailor user interfaces, and provide context-aware features based on user behavior and preferences.

```
// Personalized content recommendation

func recommendContent(for user: User) -> [Content] {

// Use AI to analyze user preferences and behavior

}
```

6. Accessibility and Inclusivity

Designing with accessibility in mind is not just a trend; it's a necessity. Apps should prioritize inclusive design, ensuring that all users, including those with disabilities, can interact with the app seamlessly.

```
// VoiceOver support for accessibility

label.isAccessibilityElement = true

label.accessibilityLabel = "Welcome to our app"
```

7. Augmented Reality (AR) Integration

AR experiences are becoming more common in apps, offering innovative ways to engage users. AR can be used for gaming, virtual try-ons, and enhancing real-world experiences through the device's camera.

```
// ARKit integration for augmented reality
```

```
let arView = ARSCNView()

arView.session.run(configuration)
```

8. Sustainability and Ethical Design

Users are increasingly conscious of the environmental impact of technology. Sustainable design practices, including energy-efficient coding and ethical data handling, are gaining importance. Apps that respect user privacy and prioritize sustainability are well-received.

As iOS app developers, staying updated with these UX design trends is crucial for creating apps that resonate with users and remain competitive in the ever-evolving app market. Incorporating these trends into your app development process can lead to a more engaging and user-friendly experience for your audience.

Section 20.4: App Security and Privacy

Ensuring the security and privacy of user data is a paramount concern in iOS app development. Users trust apps with their personal information, and any breach of that trust can have serious consequences. In this section, we'll explore the key considerations and best practices for app security and privacy.

1. Data Encryption

Data encryption is fundamental to protecting sensitive information. iOS provides tools like the CommonCrypto library to implement encryption for data at rest and data in transit. It's crucial to encrypt user data, especially when it's stored on the device or transmitted over the network.

```
// Encrypting sensitive data
```

```
let encryptedData = try? data.encrypt(using: .aes, key: encryptionKey)
```

2. Secure Authentication

Implement secure authentication mechanisms, such as biometrics (Touch ID or Face ID) and strong, unique passwords. Avoid storing passwords in plain text and use secure storage options like the Keychain for sensitive credentials.

```
// Biometric authentication

let context = LAContext()

context.evaluatePolicy(.deviceOwnerAuthenticationWithBiometrics, localizedReason: "Unlock to access your data") { success, error in

if success {

// User authenticated

} else {

// Authentication failed

}

}
```

3. User Data Permissions

Respect user data permissions and request only the data necessary for your app's functionality. Explain why you need access to specific data, and provide clear options for users to grant or deny permission.

```
// Requesting camera access

AVCaptureDevice.requestAccess(for: .video) { granted in
```

```
if granted {
// Camera access granted
} else {
// Camera access denied
}
}
```

4. Secure Backend

If your app communicates with a backend server, ensure that the server follows security best practices. Use secure protocols like HTTPS and implement proper authentication and authorization mechanisms.

```
// Making secure API requests
let url = URL(string: "https://api.example.com/data")
var request = URLRequest(url: url)
request.httpMethod = "GET"
let task = URLSession.shared.dataTask(with: request) { data, response, error in
// Handle API response securely
}
task.resume()
```

5. Data Minimization

Collect and store only the data necessary for your app's core functionality. Avoid excessive data collection and regularly review your data retention policies.

```
// Collecting minimal user data

struct UserProfile {

let username: String

let email: String

// Other necessary properties

}
```

6. Privacy Policy

Create a clear and accessible privacy policy that explains how user data is collected, used, and protected. Make it easy for users to access the policy within the app.

7. Regular Security Audits

Conduct regular security audits and vulnerability assessments to identify and address potential security weaknesses. Stay updated with security patches and updates for third-party libraries.

8. User Consent

Obtain informed consent from users regarding data collection and usage. Allow users to opt in or out of data tracking and sharing.

9. Legal Compliance

Stay informed about relevant privacy laws and regulations, such as GDPR and CCPA, and ensure that your app complies with them. Seek legal counsel if necessary.

10. Data Breach Response Plan

Have a well-defined plan in place to respond to data breaches promptly and transparently. Notify affected users and authorities as required by law.

Protecting user data and privacy is an ongoing process that requires vigilance and a commitment to best practices. By implementing these security and privacy measures, you not only protect your users but also build trust, which is essential for the long-term success of your iOS app.

Section 20.5: Building for the Future of iOS

The landscape of iOS development is ever-evolving, and staying up-to-date with the latest trends and technologies is essential for building successful apps. In this section, we'll explore the future trends in iOS development and how you can prepare your app for the challenges and opportunities that lie ahead.

1. Swift Evolution

Swift, the programming language for iOS development, continues to evolve. Stay informed about the latest Swift features and updates. Apple regularly introduces improvements that can enhance your app's performance and codebase.

// Swift 6 introduces new concurrency features

```
async {
let data = await fetchData()
// Handle data asynchronously
}
```

2. Cross-Platform Development

Consider cross-platform development frameworks like SwiftUI and Flutter. These frameworks allow you to write code once and deploy it on both iOS and Android platforms, potentially reducing development time and effort.

```
// SwiftUI for cross-platform UI development
struct ContentView: View {
var body: some View {
Text("Hello, world!")
}
}
```

3. Machine Learning and AI

Integrate machine learning and artificial intelligence into your apps to provide personalized experiences and intelligent features. Core ML makes it easier than ever to leverage machine learning models.

```
// Core ML for image recognition
let model = try? VNCoreMLModel(for: MyImageClassifier().model)
```

```
let request = VNImageRequestHandler(ciImage: image)

try? request.perform([VNCoreMLRequest(model: model)]) { response, error in

// Process ML results

}
```

4. Augmented Reality (AR)

Augmented reality experiences are gaining popularity. ARKit enables you to create immersive and interactive AR apps. Explore AR for gaming, shopping, education, and more.

```
// ARKit for augmented reality experiences

let arView = ARView(frame: .zero)

let configuration = ARWorldTrackingConfiguration()

arView.session.run(configuration)
```

5. IoT Integration

The Internet of Things (IoT) is expanding rapidly. Consider integrating your app with IoT devices to offer users control and automation capabilities.

```
// Control smart home devices

let thermostat = SmartThermostat()

thermostat.setTemperature(22.5)
```

6. Privacy-Focused Design

Privacy will remain a central concern. Continue to prioritize user data protection and transparency in your app's design and development.

7. App Clips

App Clips allow users to access small parts of your app quickly. Implement App Clips for seamless interactions and user acquisition.

8. Accessibility and Inclusivity

Ensure your app is accessible to users with disabilities. Apple's accessibility features continue to expand, making it easier to create inclusive experiences.

9. Security

Stay vigilant against evolving security threats. Regularly update your app to address vulnerabilities and ensure user data remains secure.

10. 5G Connectivity

As 5G networks become more widespread, consider optimizing your app for faster data transfer and lower latency, opening up new possibilities for real-time experiences.

11. Sustainability

Consider the environmental impact of your app. Optimize for energy efficiency and reduce unnecessary resource consumption.

12. User-Centric Design

Put users at the center of your design decisions. Continuously gather feedback and iterate on your app's user interface and experience.

The future of iOS development holds exciting opportunities for innovation and creativity. By keeping an eye on these trends and embracing new technologies, you can position your app for success and provide valuable experiences to users in the evolving iOS ecosystem.

www.ingramcontent.com/pod-product-compliance
Lightning Source LLC
Chambersburg PA
CBHW021140160726
47994CB00001B/29

* 9 7 9 8 2 2 3 1 2 0 5 2 0 *